W9-BTE-622

FLOCK TOGETHER

FLOCK

B.J. HOLLARS

TOGETHER

A Love Affair with Extinct Birds

UNIVERSITY OF NEBRASKA PRESS | LINCOLN AND LONDON

© 2017 by the Board of Regents
of the University of Nebraska
All rights reserved
Manufactured in the United
States of America

Library of Congress Cataloging-
in-Publication Data
Names: Hollars, B. J., author.
Title: Flock together: a love affair
with extinct birds / B.J. Hollars.
Description: Lincoln: University
of Nebraska Press, 2016 | Includes
bibliographical references.

Identifiers:
LCCN 2016020648 (print)
LCCN 2016044153 (ebook)
ISBN 9780803296428 (cloth: alk. paper)
ISBN 9780803296565 (epub)
ISBN 9780803296572 (mobi)
ISBN 9780803296589 (pdf)
Subjects: LCSH: Extinct birds.
| Birds—Extinction.
Classification:
LCC QL676.8 .H65 2016 (print)
| LCC QL676.8 (ebook)
| DDC 598.168—dc23
LC record available at
https://lccn.loc.gov/2016020648

Set in Garamond Premier
by John Klopping.
Designed by N. Putens.

To the birds we've lost,
and the people who tried
to save them.

For one species to mourn
the death of another is a
new thing under the sun.

—ALDO LEOPOLD, "On a
Monument to the Pigeon," 1947

CONTENTS

ACKNOWLEDGMENTS

While birding is, on occasion, a solitary pursuit, writing about birds certainly isn't.

I am indebted to so many who've taught me so much, including (but certainly not limited to) Larry Bennett, Dana Ehret, Josh Engel, Paula Holahan, Mark Lefebvre, Dave Linderud, Sumner Matteson, Jane Weinke, Dr. Stanley Temple, Dr. David Blockstein, Dr. Curt Meine, Joel Greenberg, and Julie Betchkal.

Most of all, thanks to Steve Betchkal, who allowed me to join his flock at a time when I hardly knew what a flock was. Without Steve, there would be no book, and unquestionably, far fewer birds in my life.

Thanks also to the Leigh Yawkey Woodson Art Museum, the Alabama Museum of Natural History, the Field Museum of Natural History, the University of Wisconsin–Madison's Department of Zoology, and the James Newman Clark Bird Museum, all of which opened their doors (and specimen drawers) wide for me.

Thanks to the many writers, scholars, birders, and ornithologists who came before. Too many to name, to be sure, though perhaps I might at least acknowledge a few who have helped brings these birds to life for me. Folks such as Christopher Cokinos, Stephen Lyn Bales, Phillip Hoose, Michael Steinberg, Tim Gallagher, Dr. John Fitzpatrick, Ron Rohrbaugh, Pat Leonard, Dr. Jerome Jackson, Noel Snyder, and many others.

Thanks, too, to the people who first published portions of this book, including Jon Chopan, Jason Smith, Erika Janik, Erica Trabold, Chuck Heikkinen, Delia Unson, Claire Kortnya, Mary-Kim Arnold, Nick Meyer, Tom Giffey, Eric Christenson, and Mike Paulus.

Thanks to all my inspiring students, and in particular, my student assistants: Josh Bauer, Alex Long, David Hammersborg, Joe Thunstrom, Jamie Utphall, and Winnie Khaw—all of whom sifted through history so that I might better understand these birds in the context of their time. Additionally, thanks to my former student Brady Krien, whose insights on the natural world—not to mention his canoeing prowess— helped me understand what I mightn't have otherwise.

Thanks to my friends and colleagues at the University of Wisconsin– Eau Claire, and in particular, Chancellor James Schmidt, Provost Patricia Kleine, President Kimera Way, Dean David Leaman, Dean Carmen Manning, Dr. Erica Benson, Dr. Audrey Fessler, Dr. David Jones, Dr. Stephanie Turner, Max Garland, Jon Loomis, Allyson Loomis, Molly Patterson, John Hildebrand, Greg Kocken, Nick Butler, Dr. Justin Patchin, Dr. Jason Spraitz, Dr. Paula Kleintjes Neff, Dr. Chris Floyd, Dr. Paul Thomas, Lynn Janik, and Joanne Erickson. I could go on.

Thank you to Patricia and Bernard "Duffy" Duyfhuizen as well, whose Duyfhuizen Professorship in English provided me the financial support to seek these birds to the best of my ability.

In addition, thank you to Dr. Karen Havholm and the Office of Research and Sponsored Programs at the University of Wisconsin– Eau Claire, whose University Research and Creative Activity grant also proved vital to this project.

Thank you to Brendan Todt, whose correspondence and friendship helped me see beyond the feathers.

To the Wait! What? Writers for your fellowship and feedback.

And finally, a thank you to my family—all rare birds themselves—who not only put up with me, but joined me in craning our necks toward the sky.

Excerpts from this book have been previously published or featured in a variety of publications and media outlets, all of which are listed below alongside their original titles.

"Blood Feathers," *Prime Number*
"A Field Guide to Extinction," *45th Parallel*
"The Hermit and the Hawk," *The Rumpus*
"The Resurrection of the Lord God Bird," *Wisconsin People &
Ideas*
"A Tribute to the Passenger Pigeon," *Wisconsin Life, Passenger
Pigeon, Flyway*
"What Made a Wisconsin Naturalist Want to Disappear?,"
Volume One
"The Hermit and the Goshawk," *Wisconsin Life*
"The Unnatural History of Wisconsin's First Mountain Lion,"
Flyway
"Unsolved Histories: A Bird Lost, A Sketch Found, and a Dream
to Bring it Back," *Michigan Quarterly Review* online

AUTHOR'S NOTE

When writing of extinction, one finds oneself continually forced to
choose between various accounts of "last sightings." While I have
selected 1944 as the last confirmed American sighting of the Ivory-billed
Woodpecker, others might point to a number of other possibilities,
including Gene Sparling's alleged 2004 sighting, Bobby Harrison and
Tim Gallagher's alleged sighting days later, or any of the other fifteen
or so alleged sightings search teams identified between 2004 and 2005.

The story of the Ivory-billed Woodpecker becomes further complicated when we consider the Cuban Ivory-billed Woodpecker, a
subspecies of the Ivory-billed Woodpecker, whose last confirmed sighting occurred in eastern Cuba in 1987. While I have not addressed the
Cuban Ivory-billed Woodpecker herein, for those interested in learning
more, a number of fine books have been written on the subject.

Given the difficulty of confirming "last sightings"—especially where
the Ivory-billed Woodpecker is concerned—I have taken the more
conservative approach of relying upon what I believe to be the most
generally accepted information available. This is not to say that all

readers should accept this information as definitive fact, but simply to explain my choices along the way.

While extinction implies finality, on occasion it can seem a bit slippery, too. As such, should any "Lazarus species" rise up from their extinct status, I will gladly make the appropriate revisions.

I will more than gladly do so.

FLOCK TOGETHER

Prologue

DODO LOST

The Dodo used to walk around,
And take the sun and air.
The sun yet warms his native ground—
The Dodo is not there!
The voice which used to squawk and squeak
Is now for ever dumb—
Yet may you see his bones and beak
All in the Mu-se-um.
—Hilaire Belloc, "The Dodo," 1896

Had the birds not come searching for me, I might not have gone searching for them. But they did, one warm September afternoon, just as I sat down for lunch.

At first I mistook their tapping for a knock on the front door, but as I moved toward it, it was evident that the sound was coming from elsewhere.

I returned to the table, reached for my soup, when suddenly the knocking repeated:

Tap-tap-tap-tap-tap . . .

I stood at attention, peeked out the back door, and saw nothing.

Tap-tap-tap-tap-tap . . .

Turning at whiplash speed, I caught a glimpse of a small, speckled frame gripping the screen door with his claws. His tapping repeated (*Tap-tap-tap-tap-tap / Tap-tap-tap-tap-tap*), prompting me to crane my neck to get a better view.

"Woodpecker," I cried to my wife and young children, bounding over baby carriers and bouncers until reaching my phone. "We got a live one here!"

Twenty-first-century birder that I am (or had become in the days preceding my first conscious sighting), I clicked on my Audubon Birds Pro app, scrolling past everything between albatross and Wood Warbler before reaching the digital family of woodpeckers aglow on my screen. Fifth on the list were the Downies, complete with a near-identical photo of the bird I'd just encountered. There he was, white bellied and red patched and just an inch or two longer than my fist.

It's you, I thought. *You're my guy.*

Upon peering back out the window, I learned that "my guy" was only one half of a pair. A moment later his counterpart greeted me, a female Downy who blurred past my feeder, taking refuge in the backyard birch.

I didn't quite know the protocol for what to do next. The answer, I now know, is to keep quiet and enjoy the show. Bumbling birder that I was, I did the opposite.

I clicked on the app's audio feature, blasted "Whinny call #2" from my phone's speaker.

The recorded call bleated through the screen door and infiltrated my yard.

It was enough to frighten the female back into flight, though the male—more curious than scared—momentarily observed me from his nearby roost.

Our eyes locked, and then, just as quickly as he'd come, he disappeared into the trees.

That was it. That was everything.
The birds had called, and I'd answered.

When I first learned of extinction, I hardly learned of extinction at all. Instead, I learned of the phenomenon's poster child, the Dodo—a flightless, feathered, football-shaped bird that by the late 1600s had marched his pigeon-like legs into oblivion. Of course, we humans paved that trail—hunting them until their numbers dwindled, then allowing an invasive species of wild pig to finish the job.

In third-grade science class, we never quite got around to the finger pointing. Certainly there was no discussion of the relentless assaults by sailors and swine on the remote Mauritius Island. Instead, we at our desks were mostly content just staring at paintings of that silly-looking bird, a creature we never knew existed beyond the confines of Disney's *Alice in Wonderland*.

When our teacher explained to us that the Dodo was more than a movie star—that, in fact, it had once existed—her explanation managed only to spur further questions.

What did she mean by "once"? I wondered. *How could something that once existed no longer exist anywhere in the world?*

I took my teacher's claim as a challenge and, that very afternoon, wandered the woods behind my Indiana home in search of what hadn't been seen in well over three hundred years. While I spotted the usual array of midwestern avian inhabitants—a preponderance of robins and finches and crows—I was surprised to find not a single Dodo among them.

After an exhaustive fifteen-minute investigation, I faced facts: the Dodo, it seemed, did not live anywhere in my backyard.

Which proves nothing, I decided as I tromped home for dinner that night.

After all, every house on our block had a backyard—plenty of places for some silly-looking bird to hide.

To say that I was in Dodo denial would be an understatement. Frankly, I was a hell-bent nine-year-old cut from the same cloth as Ahab, motivated (at least I thought) not by some deep inner turmoil but by an innate desire to prove my teacher wrong. In retrospect, I can now admit that perhaps my struggle to grasp the Dodo's extinction was, in fact, related to my own inner turmoil; namely, my inability to come to grips with what seemed impossible, that entire species could vanish on a large scale.

If the rumors *were* true and the Dodo *was* extinct, then what prevented other species from joining them?

Of course, plenty of species have—five mass extinctions' worth—though it wasn't until nine-year-old me began pouring over my local library's collection of illustrated dinosaur books that I began to rethink my own Dodo-related doubt. It was one thing for some football-shaped bird to hide, but where the hell were all the dinosaurs?

There was no denying it; the facts were now clear.

Probably, they were hiding together.

After two decades with no signs of a Dodo, I shift my search to a slightly more accessible species: the oft thought to be extinct Ivory-billed Woodpecker. I'm well aware of my needle-in-a-haystack odds of spotting a live one, which is why I begin my search for a dead one, instead.

I first meet Dr. Dana Ehret, curator of paleontology for the Alabama Museum of Natural History, at 8:00 a.m. on a Thursday morning near the bike racks outside his office. I'd returned to my graduate school alma mater—the University of Alabama—to give a few readings, and I'd enlisted Dana's help in tracking down an Ivory-billed Woodpecker skin.

An Internet search had revealed that one might reside in the museum's collection, though in email exchanges with Dana, he explained that the specimen's lack of catalog number made it doubtful that our bird in question ever completed her trip to Tuscaloosa. And even if she had, given that she was collected in 1866—just a year removed from the university's burning at the hands of the Union army—it was unlikely her carefully preserved skin had remained so on into the present day.

"Still," he wrote in reply, "we can have a look."

Shortly after our introduction, I follow the thirty-five-year-old bespectacled curator to the third floor of Mary Harmon Bryant Hall, at which point he leads me toward a double-wide wooden doorway.

A beep and a key-turn later the doors are flung wide, revealing a concrete, temperature-controlled room, which, to my eyes, resembles the world's most extravagant bomb shelter.

"This is the collections storage area," Dana says, refuting my bomb shelter theory. "We've got everything from taxidermied bears and lions to shoes and dolls. Even a shrunken head."

He leads me through the compact storage shelves, opening and closing each row to reveal the array of oddities and treasures within. There's the taxidermy row (complete with everything from black bears to barracudas), followed by the art row (portraits of naturalists and librarians, just to name a few). A bit farther down we reach the storage drawers, each of them filled with a spectrum of specimens.

Dana climbs a ladder, then removes the sliding drawer featuring the woodpeckers.

"So here we have our five Pileated Woodpeckers," he says, holding the drawer before me.

I stare at the flock of faded specimens, each aligned neatly alongside the next. They appear perfectly preserved, their wings folded tight to the shells of their bodies, a conga line of creatures facing beak to back.

"No Ivory-bill, though," Dana admits, reaching for the nearest Pileated to search its secondary feathers for the requisite white markings and coming up short.

Each bird is carefully tagged with a species type, a collection location, a date, and a catalog number.

But of all the specimens we'll see that day, we'll find no Ivory-billed Woodpecker.

Even dead, she's managed to elude me.

As consolation, Dana directs me to the mammoth tooth from Siberia ("Go ahead, you can touch it"), the fossil fractures ("Pretty cool, right?"), and finally, the collection's rare mosasaur bones.

"So what were these guys?" I ask, staring at what resembles a larger version of a crocodile skull.

"Mosasaurs were marine animals that lived about seventy-five to eighty million years ago," Dana explains. "They went extinct around the age of the dinosaurs."

"What happened?"

"Well, that's a debate," he says. "Did they go out with the asteroid impact along with the other dinosaurs, or right before? We aren't certain, but there are plenty of clues left behind."

He reaches forward to touch the skull, the snout, a bit of the jaw, and then begins reading the bones like a book. He takes me back seventy-five million years, to a time when this very mosasaur darted across the ancient Alabama oceans, snagging fish between its razor-sharp teeth.

"Oh, and see this?" he asks, pointing to a slight protrusion on the skull. "This looks like a healed wound. Maybe there was a fight, maybe two mosasaurs were biting each other."

I lift an eyebrow.

"You got all that from a couple of bones?"

"Sure," he smiles. "There's always something to learn from the clues."

And it's Dana's job to preserve the clues, no matter how large, small, or seemingly abundant.

"This is the part that I think is really important," he tells me. "When kids come in and see trays of dead opossums, they think, 'Why do we need trays of dead opossums?' Well, the truth is, maybe we don't need trays of dead opossums. But when we talk about things like Ivory-billed Woodpeckers, and extinction more generally, it's important to look at the historical range of these animals and how they lived. And how can we do that without collections like this? These collections," he says, "help us make projections for the future."

And as Dana makes clear, the collection's crystal-ball effect extends well beyond opossums and woodpeckers.

"Ultimately, it's about us, too. And all of this," he says, waving his arm toward the rows of specimens. "This might be more important than ever given humans' impact on the planet over the past fifty years."

"It's bad?" I ask, anticipating his answer.

"Unprecedented. And it's important that we know how mammals responded to an almost instantaneous jump in temperature because . . . well, we're going to see that again."

I don't have to ask which mammals he's most concerned about. I can see the fear in his eyes.

Since ancient times, we've begged the birds for clues. We have a name for it, augury—the practice in which augurs scanned the skies to seek answers from the flight patterns of birds. If there was a question of whether or not to go to war or pass a law, augurs were sought for their guidance. The ancients didn't believe the birds themselves had the answers, but that they served as intermediaries for the gods.

These days, select species of birds offer us insight in a different manner, mainly by not being seen at all.

Such as the aforementioned Ivory-billed Woodpecker, whose last universally confirmed U.S. sighting occurred in a Louisiana swamp in the spring of 1944. Though the species' alleged reemergence caused quite a stir in 2005, many experts have since resigned themselves to the likelihood of the bird's extinction. Yet since we can't say for certain it's gone for good, for conservation-status purposes it's listed as "critically endangered."

Other modern era birds have earned the more irreversible status, among them—in reverse chronological order of their extinction—the Carolina Parakeet (officially declared extinct in 1939), the Heath Hen (1932), the Passenger Pigeon (1914), the Labrador Duck (1878), and the Great Auk (1844 or 1852, depending on whom you ask). It's only natural to feel funereal over such a litany, though our feelings won't bring these birds back. However, it's my hope that by being made aware of the birds we've lost, we might also become aware of humanity's role in losing them.

Let the record show that I am no augur, no conservation activist, not even much of a student of science. Ask me about the periodic table and I'll ask you where you'd like me to sit. Additionally, when it comes to environmental consciousness, I'm as guilty as any other faucet-dripping, electricity-burning, gas-guzzling citizen of the industrialized world. I've likely chugged more than my fair share of soda out of Styrofoam cups, as well as tossed more than a few plastic forks into campfires. I admit also—rather embarrassingly—that I'm a halfhearted recycler at best, and though I participate in the weekly ritual of sorting trash from what only appears to be trash, I've often wondered if the process was concocted simply to distract me from creating more trash.

The point being: we needn't be as green as a forest glade to understand what we've lost and keep losing. Likewise, we needn't be card-carrying members of Greenpeace or the Sierra Club to understand the world in which we live. I'm proof that anyone with a willingness to learn can, and arguably should, participate in the critical environmental debates of our time. After all, we are all stakeholders in protecting our planet—a line so painfully obvious that it hardly seems worth writing. Yet I do because for many of us, guardianship of our world remains unconscionably low on our daily priority list.

Why worry about tomorrow, we think, *when we're busy living today?*

Indeed, we humans *are* busy living today, though this luxury doesn't extend to all species.

I refer you to the Heath Hen, the Passenger Pigeon, the Ivory-bill itself.

In *Hope Is the Thing with Feathers*, author Christopher Cokinos describes the "causation" leading to extinction as a "complex unwinding rope that we have to weave back together, even if many strands are missing." Throughout the writing of this book, I've learned that people like Dana Ehret do a lot of that weaving. But so do men like James Tanner, A. W. "Bill" Schorger, Francis Zirrer, Aldo Leopold, Don Eckelberry, Frank Chapman, and so many others from the recent past, all of whom fought fiercely to save or preserve bird species as they continued to drift away. In many instances, knowledge of these men's contributions has drifted away as well, an error I hope to correct throughout this book.

More-contemporary people deserve praise, too, such as Steve Betchkal, Joel Greenberg, Dr. Curt Meine, Dr. David Blockstein, Dr. Stanley Temple, Josh Engel, and the phalanx of ornithologists, conservationists, and scientists from the Cornell Lab of Ornithology, the Nature Conservancy, the Audubon Society, the Department of Natural Resources, the U.S. Fish and Wildlife Service, and the Environmental Protection Agency, among many other organizations that strive to educate the public on environmental issues pertinent to our daily lives. These people and organizations have taken their conservation message from schoolyards to backyards and everywhere in between, dutifully raising awareness of the environmental challenges of our time, while reminding us, too, that our time to overcome these challenges is limited.

While men primarily populate this book, women, too, have played vital roles in furthering the environmental message. From *Silent Spring* author Rachel Carson to bird advocate Rosalie Edge, women's contributions are undoubtedly noteworthy, and their stories deserve their own book. However, throughout the writing of this work, I found myself gravitating more toward the stories of men; men who—try as they might—watched as one species after another slipped between their fingers.

Allow me to close with a reality that is often overlooked: though the story of extinction is often tragic, it is also a natural, biological occurrence.

What's less natural, however, is the rate at which we are dispensing of species.

Citing Eric Chivian and Aaron Bernstein's *Sustaining Life*, the Center for Biological Diversity notes that the normal extinction rate is approximately "one to five species per year." Today, however, some scientists believe we're "losing species at 1,000 to 10,000 times" the normal rate, describing the crisis as "the worst spate of species die-offs since the loss of the dinosaurs 65 million years ago."

I hope these numbers give you pause. They should.

And they raise a question: how do we humans avoid a similar fate?

We can begin by acknowledging that we are often the cause of the trouble, the pestilence and the scourge. Or at least we might concede our complicity as a result of our growing inattention. Given the glut of newspaper articles on the subject, I'd assumed Americans were more concerned about environmental threats than ever before. Not so, according to a 2015 Gallup poll. In fact, we Americans are less concerned about environmental issues than we were in 2014. Speaking specifically to the subject of extinction of plant and animal species, those surveyed confirmed a 5 percent drop in interest, from 41 percent to 36 percent.

Which leads us to another question: how can we be stewards for species in decline, when our interest is in decline as well?

It's easy to grow frustrated by these facts; far harder, however, is finding real-world solutions for the troubles we now face. As noted previously (see my admission of halfhearted recycling and usage of Styrofoam cups), I write this not from any ivory-towered pedestal but from my cheap seats here on the ground—the place where we all live and learn.

Though I don't have the answers, I do have the questions. And I have the stories, too: stories of people who've dedicated their lives to birds, as well as stories of birds that, even in death, offered us a message for our future.

The question now is whether we'll unplug our ears long enough to hear their message.

And if so, what might we learn from the absence of their song?

PART I

Glimpsing

1

The Resurrection of the Lord God Bird

Nature is little concerned with the fate of the individual, but there is no greater tragedy in the scheme of things than the extinction of a species.
—Don Eckelberry, "Search for the Rare Ivorybill," 1961

Once upon a time there lived a bird and then that bird stopped living.

In fact, all of those birds stopped living. They were here, then they weren't, and then, one day many years later, they were believed to be here again.

Which concludes the abridged version of the life and times of the Ivory-billed Woodpecker, a creature whose flirtations with extinction have left more than a few birding guides in flux.

Do we include it? Do we not include it? the editors wonder, though most of them often do. Or at least they offer some token mention of the bird, even if that mention generally includes the phrase "thought-to-be" or "most likely" followed by the word "extinct."

Like so many others, my introduction to the Ivory-billed Woodpecker occurred in the aftermath of its alleged rediscovery in an Arkansas swamp in 2004–5. Prior to that, I knew it only as the one that got away: the winged creature in the photograph, the skin in the drawer, the painting in the Audubon book. In my mind it was always a lifeless thing, some relic from a distant past. Though in truth, the Ivory-bills' presence is hardly distant, and there are, at least conceivably, folks still alive today for whom the memory of the bird remains fresh.

It is, after all, a memorable bird. I refer you to the work of British-born naturalist Mark Catesby, who traveled to America both in 1712 and in 1722, committing several years to documenting the country's flora and fauna. In the book that resulted—*The Natural History of Carolina, Florida and the Bahama Islands*—Catesby dedicates a full page to the Ivory-bill, which he refers to as "the Largest White-bill Woodpecker." His description notes the bird's weight ("twenty ounces"), its bill ("white as ivory"), and its general coloring (mostly black, a bit of white, as well as the male's trademark "large peaked crest of scarlet feathers").

Catesby's description is my scholarly entry point into the Ivory-billed Woodpecker, though of more interest to me is his accompanying sketch, perhaps the world's first visual depiction of the bird.

There he is gripping tight to the bark of a willow oak, his beak perpetually frozen, forever preparing for the knock. His eye is a trifecta of concentric circles: the yellow sclera circling the black iris circling the white pupil. And of course there is the scarlet torch atop his head, confirmation of his maleness.

Over half a century later, naturalist Alexander Wilson further contributed to our current understanding of the memorable bird. In addition to his talents as a naturalist and illustrator, the Scottish-born Wilson was a poet, too, proof of which is confirmed in his vaunted descriptions of the Ivory-billed Woodpecker, which he deemed the "chief of his tribe" and the "head of the whole class of Woodpeckers." Wilson's unbridled enthusiasm for the Ivory-bill continues for several pages throughout his book, whose unwieldy title, *American Ornithology; or, The Natural History of the Birds of the United States: Illustrated with Plates, Engraved and Coloured from Original Drawings Taken from Nature*, seems to have adopted the form of the epic rather than the haiku.

Yet the persevering reader is rewarded with far more succinct descriptions of the birds themselves, many of which still contribute to our modern understanding of species' behaviors. This is especially true of the Ivory-bill, which Wilson encountered firsthand in the winter of 1809.

On that fateful day as he roamed the North Carolina forests in search of birds, he spotted a young male perched in a tree. Since he had yet to sketch this particular species, he acted as any nineteenth-century naturalist might—by lifting his gun and firing. For sketching purposes, he hoped to acquire his specimen mostly intact, though in fact did one better by acquiring him mostly alive as well.

Who can say what inspired what happened next, why a man known to wear a satchel of dead birds refused, in this instance, to finish the job.

Perhaps he was smitten by the bird's "superb carmine crest" or his "bill of polished ivory." Or perhaps he'd simply grown soft for the species he believed "impress[ed] on the mind of the examiner the most reverential ideas of the Creator."

High praise, indeed, from a man who had aimed to kill.

Though kill he could not, and instead only managed to graze the bird's wing with his bullet.

Wilson paid a price for his poor marksmanship and, upon retrieving the injured bird, was forced to endure an incessant squall "exactly resembling the violent crying of a young child."

So exact was his description that upon entering an inn in nearby Wilmington, the straight-faced landlord inquired as to whether Wilson and his "baby" desired a room for the night.

The bird's convincing impression had drawn a crowd, at which point Wilson pulled back a sheet to reveal the true source of the wailing. The screeching bird was an unexpected spectacle, and as the crowd chuckled, Wilson and his captive started up the stairs to their room. Underestimating the bird's determination to escape, Wilson momentarily left him unattended, and upon his return within an hour's time, spotted the bird pecking wildly at the wall, shedding the plaster like bark.

His escape plan foiled, the bird cried out, a sound Wilson translated as "grief."

Round two, though this time, Wilson got the better of the bird by tying a string around the creature's leg and cinching him to the table. Satisfied, Wilson set off again—this time in search of food for his new pet—though upon returning a second time, he witnessed even more havoc than before.

"As I reascended the stairs," Wilson remembered, "I heard him again hard at work, and on entering had the mortification to perceive that he had almost entirely ruined the mahogany table to which he was fastened, and on which he had wreaked his whole vengeance."

Wilson had to hand it to him—the bird had pluck—though his admiration was hardly mutual.

As he took to his sketchbook, the difficulty of his latest artistic endeavor began to set in: this was no still life with woodpecker, quite the opposite.

"While engaged in taking the drawing," Wilson wrote, "he cut me severely in several places."

Yet the bird's remarkable fight only further enhanced Wilson's admiration for him.

The creature "displayed such a noble and unconquerable spirit," Wilson remarked, "that I was frequently tempted to restore him to his native woods."

Tempted, though not convinced to act on it.

Instead, he held the bird captive for three days while perfecting his sketch, and then, once the bird's hunger strike got the better of him, Wilson "witnessed his death with regret."

Upon first reaching this place in Wilson's narrative, I shuddered and refused to read on.

I, too, found myself regretting that Ivory-bill's death, not because the bird was a rarity then, but because such a noble bird surely deserved to die with a bit more dignity.

Or at least not tethered to a table, his world just a windowpane away.

The only silver lining comes from my imaginings; a scene in which a tongue-tied Wilson explains to the landlord how his "baby" left the room in disarray.

That's one guy, I think contemptuously, *who's not getting his deposit back.*

If you're dead set on seeing an Ivory-bill, might I suggest you settle for seeing a dead one? Your odds of success are much higher, particularly given that the number of skins preserved in museums far surpasses the Ivory-bills in the trees.

Or, if you'd rather save yourself a trip, you can always limit your search to a search engine, a strategy that not only allows you to research from the comfort of your armchair but also provides the opportunity for digitized comparison between the Ivory-bill and its commonplace cousin, the Pileated Woodpecker.

At first glance, the two species appear all but indistinguishable, their similarities in size and coloring having caused more than a few misidentifications over the years. The Pileated is the Ivory-bill's spoiler, the avian world's equivalent of the man in the Bigfoot suit. I imagine that every time a member of the Ivory-bill faithful spots a Pileated, his heart begins to race. How could it not, given the birds' many similarities? Though of course they're not identical, and once the spotter's heart rate returns to normal levels, he would be best served to take a good hard look at the bird in question's underwing patterns. In this way, his determination can be as simple as black or white—a black trailing edge of feathers points to a Pileated, whereas a white trailing edge gives credence to an Ivory-bill.

Or one can take the Occam's Razor approach: If it looks like an Ivory-bill and it sounds like an Ivory-bill, chances are it's still probably a Pileated.

I don't mean to be glib, but there's simply no getting around it.

According to a 2012 report in *Conservation Biology*, the chance that the Ivory-bill has endured is 0.0064 percent, which means the odds of seeing one, as *BirdWatching*'s Matt Mendenhall writes, are about 1 in 15,625. To put that in perspective, you're about five times more likely to get struck by lightning than spot this particular bird.

(And with my luck, I'd probably get struck by lightning *while* unsuccessfully searching for an Ivory-bill.)

Which is why I encourage you, dear reader, to take the safer approach, one in which the odds are in your favor. Make do with a study skin, or an artist's depiction—both of which are better than nothing, and in the latter case, far better than nothing: the birds forever captured on canvas at the climax of their glory.

Despite the uncertainty surrounding the bird's existence, one thing remains clear: what we lack in living Ivory-bills, we more than make up for with their portraiture. John James Audubon famously painted the species, but so too did a host of other wildlife artists—Larry Chandler, Roger Tory Peterson, and Don Eckelberry, among others. Taken together, their portraits of the Ivory-billed Woodpecker provide us with an array of visual representations of the bird.

Of them, I'm most entranced by the depiction offered by the aforementioned Alexander Wilson—not exactly a deadeye with a gun, but he inarguably had an eye for art. Though admittedly, I appreciate his depiction not for any technical reasons, but because when I stare at that bird's portrait, I'm reminded of that creature's tragic tale. Specifically, that the bird Wilson preserved so well on the page he killed so poorly in life, forcing that injured animal to subsist for three days before at last succumbing to starvation.

Upon staring at the print, I can't shake the jarring disconnect between what I see and what I know to be true. For me, the version of the Ivory-bill Wilson presents seems wholly inauthentic; a version of a bird clinging to a branch, when in fact, at the time he was sketched, all that bird clung to was life.

A more accurate depiction might have revealed the remnants of the mahogany table to which he was chained, his feathers half covered in the dust of freshly pecked plaster. It might also have shown the extent of his bodily injuries, some hint of the frantic desperation in his final moments. Instead, Wilson gives us a bird on a branch, and directly above it, a zoomed headshot of the bird from the chest up.

This is the classic version, the neutered version, the fictional version, too.

Some nights when I hear a Pileated knocking on my backyard pines, my mind leaps to that room in that inn in Wilmington, to that injured bird tethered like a broken-tailed kite, kicking into the stale air while his captor hushed him, soothed him, and sketched him as fast as he could.

I'm hardly the first to romanticize the Ivory-billed Woodpecker. Even

Wilson—who let one die on his watch—praised the creature for his "dignity," his "perseverance," his "melancholy cries." Perhaps we expect nothing less from a poet turned birder, though many other naturalists and ornithologists have been equally generous in their descriptions of the Ivory-billed Woodpecker. Even its nickname—the Lord God Bird—is an indication of our reverence for it; the moniker is said to have originated due to the regularity with which the phrase "Lord God!" escaped the mouths of those lucky enough to glimpse one in the wild.

Yet over the past seventy years, few have had the opportunity to utter those words for that reason. Which is not to say that nobody has. Part of the mythos of the Lord God Bird is that it refuses to—in the words of another poet, Dylan Thomas—"go gentle into that good night."

Rather, it seems to subscribe to a whack-a-mole existence within the birding community: there one moment, gone the next, all while observers are left wondering what they've seen. Just when people begin to think it's gone for good, it returns again, taking a cue from the phoenix and rising once more from the ash.

Even today, when entering the swamps and bogs of the southern coast, some swear they can still hear it.

Not just the trumpeting *kent-kent* call of the Ivory-bill, but its human accompaniment:

Lord God, Lord God, Lord God . . .

Ornithologists speak often of the "spark bird," the one that—through its beauty or grace or other intangible quality—"sparks" one's lifetime interest in birds. It's the one that reels us in, the one that reawakens our childlike wonder, reminding us that birds are everywhere if we only bother to look.

Except for my own unconventional spark bird, whose spark—as we've already discussed—is more likely to come in the form of a lightning strike.

Fortunately for me, my quest for the Ivory-billed Woodpecker begins far from the overcast skies of a swamp. Instead, it begins in my fourth-floor office at the Wisconsin university where I work. There, in the predawn hours before the trill of college students, I crack open ornithologist James T. Tanner's 1942 seminal work, the eponymously titled *The Ivory-billed Woodpecker*, and soon find myself highlighting every other word.

My first impression is that Tanner seems a bit of an odd bird himself, though only because I know few twenty-two-year-olds so committed to a cause. Then again, few twenty-two-year-olds have the chance to study a species so close to extinction, to dedicate a combined twenty-one months to self-imposed exile in an effort to save a bird on the brink. Which is precisely what Tanner did while completing his doctoral work at Cornell University. He was encouraged by his mentor, fellow Ivory-bill scholar Arthur Allen, who saw to it that his protégé received the first Audubon Fellowship, thereby granting Tanner ample time to pursue the research both men cared deeply about—how best to save the swiftly depleting species.

Perhaps no one understood the unique challenges of preserving the Ivory-bills better than Allen. In 1924, upon hearing rumors of multiple sightings in central Florida, Allen and his wife took a road trip south and, with the help of a guide, soon stumbled upon a nesting pair in the throes of their courtship ritual. Allen described the way the birds darted from cypress to pine, how they "called and preened" from their new locale as the dawn broke into day.

"Finally," Allen wrote, "the female climbed up directly below the male and when she approached him closely he bent his head downward and clasped bills with her."

If it was a kiss, then it was a last kiss.

Within hours of the sighting, word of the birds' location had spread, and the pair was soon shot and killed.

The tragic irony, of course, is that the man who likely admired those birds most was now the one with secondhand blood on his hands.

His presence confirmed the birds' extrinsic value, proof to local hunters that if their regional species of woodpecker was good enough for a big-city scientist, surely it was worth the cost of a bullet or two.

Enter James Tanner: Allen's fresh-faced star student, not to mention the Ivory-bills' last, best chance at survival. In the introduction to Tanner's book, Allen praised his pupil for possessing "the qualities necessary for a field ornithologist," including "an ability to rough it and to get along with all types of people in all kinds of situations, a natural adaptability, ingenuity, initiative, originality, and a willingness to work."

From 1937 to 1939, Tanner would make use of all of these skills, combing over forty-five locations from the Santee Bottoms of South Carolina to the Big Thicket of Texas. Despite covering over forty-five thousand miles, his sightings remained limited to a small section of virgin timber in Louisiana's Singer Tract. Tanner—often accompanied by local guide J. J. Kuhn—dedicated months of observation to this locale and was rewarded for it. Though Tanner's sightings were limited to a handful of Ivory-bills, he was fortunate to spot them with some regularity, allowing him to gather enough data to eventually propose a set of recommendations for a conservation program.

Tanner's book spares no scientific detail, offering insight on everything from habitat to history, from courtship to caring for young. Yet in the midst of all this—buried deep in his "Care of Young" chapter—is a brief side story that forever altered my understanding of the Ivory-bill, as well as our relationship to it.

As Tanner tells it, on the morning of March 6, 1938—his twenty-fourth birthday, no less—he and Kuhn kept their eyes on a nesting tree in the Singer Tract in anticipation of banding a juvenile. Mid-morning, once mother and father Ivory-bill took to the sky, Tanner began his own upward climb in the newly spiked tree, eventually arriving at the nest.

"Just as I reached toward the entrance," Tanner wrote, "the youngster jumped, but he jumped right into my hand and I caught him."

This made for easy banding, and upon completing his task, Tanner made good use of his heightened position to remove one of the branches obscuring his view of the nesting hole.

Startled, the young bird jumped yet again, this time crashing to the ground.

"Down the tree I went, as fast as I could, and picked up the young bird," Tanner wrote. "Handing him to Kuhn, I started to take photographs of the bird."

What happened next served as fodder for more than a few of my

Ivory-bill-filled fantasies: the way Kuhn cradled the bird in his palms until the youngster pried himself free, eventually perching on Kuhn's wrist. From there, the bird (they named him Sonny Boy) skittered up Kuhn's arm, pausing on his shoulder before issuing "a few sharp taps on his cap."

Tanner's photos offer the play-by-play, each snapped photograph providing new insight on the Ivory-bills' interactions with humans. While Alexander Wilson's table-tethering approach served as one model, Kuhn's gentler interaction served as another.

Tanner's book offers just enough photos to whet my palate, and since I'm hungry for more, I gluttonously turn to the Internet. For fifteen minutes I scroll through one photo after the next, marveling at what I believe to be the first photographically documented direct encounter between a human and an Ivory-bill. What's more, despite this unprecedented intimacy, the bird in the photos shows no apparent leeriness toward Kuhn. Quite to the contrary, he appears to have transformed that man into a human perch, eventually making himself comfortable atop Kuhn's cap.

Of the many photos in the series, this is the one that best captures my imagination: that young bird holding court atop the man's cap, his beak parted as if issuing a royal decree. Though hardly the photo's focal point, Kuhn plays a convincing perch nonetheless. At least he appears as stiff as one, his head angled down while his right hand steadies his binoculars to his chest. The bill of his cap shadows his eyes, though even half shrouded, his slight smile is impossible to miss.

"When I had used all my film," Tanner later recalled, "I wrapped the young bird in two handkerchiefs, put it inside my shirt, and climbed again to the nest."

In total—from banding to the bird's safe return to the nest—the interaction lasted less than an hour. It was all the time he had for us.

From my own perch in my fourth-floor office, I study the photos awhile longer.

They offer me insight in a way the artwork can't: namely, by depicting an unplanned, unposed, and unexpected encounter between species.

But no matter how long I stare at the photos, the answer I most want to know continues to elude me:

Was that bird saying hello or goodbye?

At the conclusion of Tanner's in-depth study, he lays out five specific recommendations to ensure the continuation of the species. Of them, the most vital encourages lumber companies—in the case of the Singer Tract, the Chicago Lumber Company—to adopt more selective logging practices. Specifically, he hoped the lumber company might consider dividing their logging tracts into three categories: logging areas, partial cutting areas, and reserve areas. In this way, Tanner believed, lumber companies could continue their harvest while preserving the rare birds' habitat.

It seemed a reasonable enough request: spare some trees and spare a species, too. So reasonable, in fact, that Audubon Society president John Baker immediately embraced the recommendation and began bending every ear he could—from President Roosevelt's to Secretary of the Interior Harold Ickes's, as well as contacting representatives from both the National Park Service and the U.S. Fish and Wildlife Service. Finally, he solicited help from the governors of Tennessee, Mississippi, and Arkansas as well, all of whom agreed to write letters to the Chicago Lumber Company urging them to renegotiate their land lease deal. To sweeten the potential deal, Louisiana governor Sam Jones offered the lumber company $200,000 of state money to purchase as much land as he could.

Despite this legion of support, in December 1943, when Baker and his conservation-minded colleagues attempted to broker the deal, Baker's offer was quickly dismissed. The company had been clear-cutting the land since 1938 and didn't intend to quit on account of a bird.

"We are just money grubbers," the chairman was said to have famously replied.

After legislative efforts proved equally unsuccessful, Baker tried for the Hail Mary—dispatching Audubon staffer Richard Pough to the Singer Tract, hopeful that a sighting might renew public interest.

From early December 1943 to mid-January 1944, Pough continued the search, eventually spotting only a lone, female Ivory-bill. It was an astonishing find, especially given that Tanner himself hadn't spotted one in that tract in over two years.

There, among the cypress trees, Pough observed the bird for hours as the rain fell down all around him. After she finally left—after he'd watched that bird scale the bark on the second-growth trees as a result of the shortage of old growths—Pough posited his own theory on the Ivory-bill's struggle to exist.

"Can't help feeling that mystery of I-bs disappearance is not as simple as Jim [Tanner]'s report might lead one to believe," his letter to Baker began. "I wonder if the bird's psychological requirements aren't at bottom of matter rather than it being just a matter of food."

Psychological requirements? I wonder upon reading Pough's words. Did he mean the birds' loyalty to their land?

That the Ivory-bills refused to leave their habitat, even as their habitat left them?

Of course, the decline of a species is rarely so simple a story. There are often plot twists and red herrings to consider, or at least the occasional unexpected turn. Though habitat loss is widely considered to be the ultimate cause of the Ivory-bills' demise, as many scholars have posited, there are many proximate causes to consider as well. Christopher Cokinos notes a number of them—"nest infestation by mites, inbreeding and scattered populations"—all of which may have served to metaphorically kick the bird while it was already down.

In "'Home in the Big Forest': Decline of the Ivory-Billed Woodpecker and Its Habitat in the United States," writer Mikko Saikku offers a few additional theories. While the Chicago Lumber Company's unapologetic prowess with mechanized logging practices did the birds no favors, Saikku points fingers in other directions as well: from honeybees (which may have proved a source of competition for the birds' nesting holes) to American appetites ("Ever since colonial times," Saikku writes, "the ivory-billed woodpecker had been an easy and palatable target for the hunter").

Be it by ax or by appetite, we humans unquestionably played a role in their demise, as is true of many of our recently departed birds. Saikku does not mince words: "Humans have greatly increased the rate of avian extinctions," he writes, "and thus the average longevity of a bird species has been dramatically reduced."

At the conclusion of Pough's six-week stint in the Singer Tract, he confirmed the dramatic reduction of the species, informing Baker that he was "reasonably sure" he'd found the last of the Ivory-billed Woodpeckers. Thus Baker's Hail Mary seemed to have inadvertently further doomed the already doomed bird. After all, unless there was an unobserved Mr. Ivory-Bill haunting those trees, the lone female was destined to expire with no chance for reproduction.

Switching strategies, Baker drew up a new play: this one focused on preserving the bird the only way he knew how.

He enlisted the help of another young Audubon staffer, twenty-three-year-old Don Eckelberry, whom he sent to the tract to draw a few pre-postmortem sketches of the bird.

Eckelberry was no stranger to the Ivory-bill, his first encounter occurring a decade or so prior when the young boy stared at a specimen donated to the Louisiana Department of Conservation.

"It was a big woodpecker," Eckelberry recalled years later, "larger than a crow, strikingly patterned black and white, with a long scarlet crest and a prodigious ivory-white beak."

What Eckelberry didn't know then was that in 1944 he would come in contact with another Ivory-bill—this one wild and alive. As a result of his later sighting, he would claim the dubious honor of being the last person in the United States to have a universally accepted sighting of the species.

Sketch tools in tow, Eckelberry arrived in Louisiana in early April 1944, anxious to fulfill his charge. Though upon his arrival, Pough's recommended guide, Jesse Laird, informed Eckelberry that the lumber company had recently cut down the bird's roost tree, as well as all other habitable trees in the area. The good news, Laird reported, was that he'd recently spotted the bird near her former roosting tree, and with some luck, they might find her there in the coming days.

Demoralized but not defeated, soon after his arrival, Eckelberry took refuge on the back porch belonging to his temporary host, a Louisianan he pseudonymously named "Mr. Henry." In Eckelberry's essay on his time in the tract, he wrote of an evening shared on Mr. Henry's porch, a moment in which the men watched the deer emerge from the darkened forest, their "white-lined ears twitching" while their tails "flash[ed] up like a white flag of surrender to apprehension."

"Never get tired watchin' them deer," Mr. Henry informed Eckelberry, "though they eat up the grass somethin' fierce."

Eckelberry offered no reply, though given the circumstances that led him to Louisiana, I can't help but wonder if such a statement caused him to bite his lip.

I wonder if Eckelberry thought to himself, *The deer aren't the invaders, we are*—a truth that surely resonated all too well to the last Ivory-bill asleep in her tree.

"Throw up a handful of feathers," Charles Darwin wrote, "and all must fall to the ground according to definite laws." But how are we to act when we don't yet know the penalties for the laws we're breaking, or, as Darwin put it, the "action and reaction of the innumerable plants and animals" fast fading from our world?

These days, it's a well-known fact that upon disrupting one community in an ecosystem, we risk disrupting the ecosystem at large. For the layperson such as myself, perhaps it's useful to think of ecosystems as nature's version of Jenga: when you remove one piece, you put the whole at risk. It's not only an apt metaphor, but a pedagogical activity adopted in schools throughout the country, the popular stacking game serving as a hands-on approach to helping students understand the fragile balance of life. As with Jenga, not every ecological piece removed from an ecosystem spells immediate disaster, though the more pieces removed, the weaker the ecosystem becomes. In the summer of 1869, long before the advent of Jenga, naturalist John Muir came to a similar conclusion: "When we try to pick out anything by itself," he wrote, "we find it hitched to everything else in the Universe."

By 1944 the Ivory-billed Woodpecker was indeed hitched to her diminished habitat, prompting Eckelberry—at Baker's behest—to commit two weeks to tracking her, writing and sketching every last detail he could. He went where she went—taking a boat upriver past Alligator Bayou, then a car to John's Bayou, and finally loitering around the roost tree, his ear cocked and awaiting the sound of her call.

At 6:33 p.m. on April 5, as the Barred Owls hooted in anticipation of their evening hunt, their calls were interrupted by another sound. Laird and Eckelberry froze, awaiting confirmation of what they thought they'd heard.

And suddenly there it was: an unmistakable note, then a rap, echoing through the trees.

For fourteen minutes the men heard her, anxiously awaiting her grand entrance.

Finally, amid the Downies and the Red-bellieds, at last came the long-awaited woodpecker, her wings, according to Eckelberry, "cleaving the air in strong, direct flight" as she "alighted with one magnificent upward swoop."

But in a less heroic description he also made note of her "hysterical pale eyes" and her "frantic aliveness"—descriptions more haunting than the sketches themselves.

Perhaps the Singer Tract itself was haunted, and its bird its breathing ghost. Mr. Henry's cook—a woman named Liza—surely seemed to think so, warning Eckelberry never to leave the house after dark since the woods were "full of 'ha[u]nts.'"

"But the only spirit I could hear," Eckelberry reflected years later, "was the voice of doom for this entire natural community, epitomized by that poor lone ivorybill . . . and vocalized by the shrill squeals of the donkey engine which worked all night bringing out the logs."

Eckelberry's mention of the donkey engine serves as a reminder that he and Laird were hardly alone in the woods. In fact, the loggers themselves surrounded them, many of whom were German prisoners of war under close guard, and thus far removed from their own natural habitats. German POWs were hardly rare in wartime, the United States maintaining well over four hundred thousand on American soil by the conclusion of World War II. While some were enlisted to work the land, others were enlisted to destroy it. For Eckelberry, watching the latter was almost too much to bear.

"I watched one tree come screaming down," Eckelberry wrote, "and cared to see no more."

His lament is echoed in the painting that resulted.

Upon first viewing it, I admit I'm surprised by what I see. While I'd grown accustomed to the more traditional interpretations of the bird—generally a yellowed-eyed, crimson-crested creature—Eckelberry's version hardly highlights the Ivory-bills' more memorable characteristics. Instead, the lone bird is pushed to the background, while in the foreground, the viewer is forced to witness the forest cut and thinned.

Though Baker had sent him to preserve the bird, Eckelberry mostly preserved the bird's disappearing habitat instead: a stark portrait of the refuge we'd ravaged, a reminder of the home we'd destroyed.

2

The Death List

If I could not immerse myself in bird song, I would be haunted by the echo of it.
—Steve Betchkal, "Personal Extinction," in *Make Birds Not War*, 2011

Whether or not the Ivory-billed Woodpecker is extinct is still a matter of debate. Less debatable, however, are the many other birds we've lost throughout modern history. Such as the aforementioned Heath Hen, the Carolina Parakeet, and the Passenger Pigeon, just to name a few.

While I admit to feeling little connection to some of these birds, it's hard not to feel close to Passenger Pigeons, particularly when staring at a pair from a distance of a few feet away. Which is indeed my vantage point while peering into a diorama featuring the birds in the James Newman Clark Bird Museum in my home of Eau Claire, Wisconsin.

Don't be fooled by its name; though technically a "museum," most would consider it a permanent exhibition on steroids, one whose 530 or so birds have remained frozen on shelves and in cabinets for nearly one hundred years. Donated to the University of Wisconsin–Eau Claire in 1959, the collection is currently housed in the Phillips Science Hall, a museum in the round whose center we've filled with a planetarium. Thus the bird museum is its own orbit, flocks of feathers quite literally circling the manufactured stars.

Though the museum is just a few hundred paces from my office in the English Department, I'd rarely found reason to go there. That changed at the start of the school year, once my spark bird reignited the fire within.

It wasn't all the Ivory-bill's doing.

In the fall of 2014, as we commemorated the one-hundredth anniversary of the extinction of the Passenger Pigeon, renewed public interest greeted the long-gone birds. Suddenly the pink-breasted, gray-feathered Passenger Pigeons were everywhere again, not exactly clouding the skies, but reappearing in magazines, newspapers, and documentaries, their red eyes (now marbles) staring longingly into a future that was not theirs.

Suffice it to say that I, too, was swept up in the excitement.

Mornings before class I'd regularly find myself slipping inside the museum's front doors, taking a moment of tranquility among the birds before the day's bombardment began. Working counterclockwise, I'd study the faded faces of the Golden Eagle and the goshawk, examine every last grackle and grouse. Eventually I'd make my way to the Pileated Woodpeckers—the Ivory-bills' imperfect stunt doubles—and wonder, *When will you, too, vanish from this earth?*

After several early morning walks around the museum, my eyes eventually fell to a name on a placard that didn't belong to a bird: Steve Betchkal—a birder, multimedia journalist, and from what I could gather, the museum's unofficial tour guide.

Throughout the city, his reputation preceded him; every casual conversation I had about birds somehow always circled back to Steve.

"Have you talked to him?" a longtime resident asked me. "You simply must. Sooner rather than later."

Which is how I find myself in the James Newman Clark Bird Museum on a warm October afternoon between classes.

Though enraptured by the Passenger Pigeons, I drift back toward the doors just as Steve enters.

"Hi," he greets, offering his hand. "You must be B.J."

Even if I'd somehow managed not to be intimidated by his vast knowledge, his imposing figure leaves me flustered. Measuring in at a shade over six feet tall and with a runner's frame, he appears a bit flamingo-like in posture.

And if he's the flamingo in this scenario, I think, *then I guess that makes me the brine shrimp.*

Thankfully, Steve Betchkal has no intention of devouring me. Rather, he's humble in his approach, anxious to answer my many questions and able to forgive me my ignorance.

"Come on," he says, welcoming me into his domain, "let me give you the tour."

I soon find myself back at the Passenger Pigeons' diorama, the pair mounted directly above their bed of plastic leaves. While the pigeons indeed claim prime real estate within the museum's curved walls, this hardly seems adequate reparation for our hunting them from billions to none.

Let me repeat: from *billions* to *none.*

It's the phrase that's become the sound bite to their saga, the hard truth that more than a few journalists and filmmakers have honed in on, and for good reason. The phrase is not only startling, but accurate, too, in its succinct summation.

By now you know the storyline:

Once upon a time there lived a bird and then that bird stopped living.

(Though in the case of the Passenger Pigeon, once upon a time there lived billions.)

Yet for Steve, the museum isn't meant to serve as some guilt-ridden stroll down memory lane, but as an opportunity to bring new life to the subject of birds, and conservation more generally. While Steve has no official affiliation with the university, this hardly prevents him from helping out when he can. For a time, Steve explains, the museum resembled little more than a dead bird repository, though he hopes his curatorial recommendations have helped transform it into an educational experience for amateurs and experts alike.

When first approached to assist, Steve enthusiastically agreed, later admitting that perhaps his enthusiasm got the better of him.

"I had so many plans we had to sort of curtail some of them," he says. "But one thing I did," he continues, nodding to the Passenger Pigeon diorama, "is add more birds."

For a moment I think he means literally—a long shot considering the Passenger Pigeons' conservation status.

"Right here in the clouds," he clarifies, tapping the glass and directing me toward a gray blur in the diorama's painted backdrop. "At first these were all just clouds," he says, "but I added these blotches, these birds."

To my mind, Steve's conversion of clouds to birds serves as a nice touch, a visual representation to help visitors comprehend the ubiquity of Passenger Pigeons prior to their extinction. Yet as Steve tells it, the museum's curator was apparently "less enthusiastic" about his artistic license.

"She didn't think that my standard of painting was up to the original," he says with a wry smile.

Steve continues his tour, leading me around the loop like a well-trained heeler as he points out bird after bird. He's excited to share them with me, though his excitement is offset by his disappointment in the quality of the aging specimens. While taxidermy is meant to extend the life of the skin—to take a dead thing and make it last forever—Steve's convinced Clark's specimens won't quite make it that long.

"Look at 'em," he sighs, nodding wearily to a few of the more battered creatures behind glass. "They're already falling apart."

Initially, I figured Clark's amateur status as a taxidermist might be to blame. As the legend goes, Clark dedicated the latter half of his life to preserving birds, a hobby (dare I say obsession?) that was said to have spurred a mental health issue or two. While I, too, might question the sanity of someone who commits so much life to dead things, a more logical explanation for Clark's hardships might well be attributed to his close proximity to arsenic—a key ingredient for taxidermists of the era and a substance that Clark used regularly in preparing his own skins.

When I'd first started reading Clark's journals the previous year, I took him, forgive me, for a loon. After all, what are we to make of a man who dedicated decades of his life to aiming, firing, stuffing, and mounting—the latter of which I imagined was performed on dark and stormy nights in the dirt-floored basement of his rural farmhouse. Though I can't confirm the dark-and-stormy-night part (or the basement, for that matter), every other part of his story remains true. Guided by little more than a few bird books and the encyclopedia, Clark, the amateur taxidermist, somehow managed to create museum-quality work, much of which—despite Steve's grumblings—has survived to this day.

While modern culture often (and unfairly) pokes fun at the perception of the "fine line" between taxidermists and psychopaths, Clark surely resided in the former camp. Eccentric, perhaps, but psychopath he was not. It's worth noting, too, that throughout the nineteenth and early twentieth centuries, taxidermy remained a primary means of scientific inquiry, with men such as President Theodore Roosevelt on down collecting specimens and creating taxidermy mounts later to be handed over to museums.

Despite hypothetically being in such good company, pragmatically speaking, Clark's daily dealings with dead things also made for dangerous company. Specifically, the unhealthy supply of arsenic previously noted, a substance I fear may have taken its toll. It's a fear seemingly further substantiated when I read a museum placard that notes Clark's "nervous breakdown."

Though upon reading the placard a bit closer, I learn that his breakdown wasn't *caused* by taxidermy, but rather "set him to the activity of shooting and mounting barnyard pests." As best I can deduce, the birds gave him renewed purpose, just as they were intended to. In a 1976 article on the "Bird Man" in the local paper, Clark's daughter explains how after her father's health began to decline his doctor urged the meticulous-minded farmer and moneylender to "take up some vocation for relaxation."

Clark interpreted the request as an excuse to keep his shotgun at the ready and, while farming, could often be seen lifting his eyes from the soil to the skies to harvest birds fluttering overhead. After a successful shot, Clark was said to "go vaulting across the meadows to the farm-house to get the specimen on ice before the skin spoiled"—his version of relaxation, apparently.

Upon delving deeper into his journals, I expect to find insight into Clark's life, but all I find are glimpses into a stultifying routine existence. Day after day, his entries repeat themselves: "Stuffing Birds and choring," "Stuffing Birds and choring," "Stuffing Birds and choring."

Of course, his daily mantra was occasionally interrupted by other tasks—there were birds to be shot, after all, and manure to be hauled—though from what I can gather, Clark appears to have dedicated many of his later years to, as he put it, stuffing birds and choring. For him, the two activities were distinct. Stuffing birds was *not* choring, but a passion he fostered regularly.

Steve and I break our gaze from the birds long enough to peer at a framed photograph of the man, the bringer of the birds and the sole reason we are standing here today.

"Sure was a dour-looking guy," Steve says, nodding to the solemn, mustachioed man staring back at us in sepia tone. "I call him Mr. Happy."

I smirk—a facial expression in perfect contrast to Clark's.

From my vantage point forty years after his death, Clark's a tough man to read. Was he driven to shoot and stuff birds out of love for them, or was it merely an excuse to take to the woods? Was he a "loon," as I hastily assumed, or far more likely, and as his placard notes, "an industrious, alert, perceptive man with apparently boundless energy." To a modern city slicker such as myself, it's easy to pigeonhole Clark as peculiar, though in many ways he's representative of a man of his time and place. Not only that, but his detailed accounts of the natural world (including a somewhat legendary attempt to study Great Horned Owl nests in subzero temperatures) confirms him as a citizen scientist of the highest order. His fascination with nature merely put him in step with others of his era. As for his commitment to "stuffing birds and choring," well, that's indeed one way to pass the time.

Though perhaps who Clark was isn't half as important as what he left behind.

"So what do we do with Clark's birds today?" I ask Steve. "I mean, how do we save what's already gone?"

"Well, it's more about preserving than saving," Steve says, "but some of them are already beyond repair. And the colors . . . I mean, just look at the warbler case." He walks me toward it. "These used to be colorful birds. Now they're pretty much just black and white. This one, for instance, this bird's a Red-faced Warbler, but you wouldn't have guessed it."

I certainly wouldn't have, though not because the specimen's been leached of color, but because I'm still identifying birds at a first-grade level, an ignorance that limits most of my IDs to robins and cardinals and crows.

"And this one should have a deep golden head," Steve sighs, pointing to what the placard informs me is a Prothonotary Warbler.

I mimic his sigh, trying to share his disappointment. But it's hard given that I've yet to see a Prothonotary Warbler in the wild and thus don't fully know what I'm missing.

In an effort to reveal I at least know something, I make mention of the Bachman's Warbler, another of the once-upon-a-time variety. A print of them hangs in my home office, which accounts for my knowledge of their existence.

"They're pretty rare these days, too, huh?" I comment, knowing full well that there hasn't been a confirmed sighting in about forty years, more or less, depending on whom you ask.

"Yeah, that's gone, that's dead," Steve says matter-of-factly. "It's not around anymore."

I lift an eyebrow, surprised by his lack of lament. But as I'll later learn, when it comes to rare and extinct birds, Steve's days of mourning are behind him. It's not that he cares too little, but that he cares too much—a human affliction as rare as the Ivory-bill.

Steve continues his tour, pointing out one faded bird after another and setting the colors straight in my head.

"Imagine this one with a deep blue," he says, "and this one with a yellow breast . . ."

I nod, take a note, imagine.

Midsentence he interrupts himself to ask me the question I've feared most.

"So," Steve says casually, "when did you start birding anyway?"

"Well," I mumble, allowing the sentence to trail, "you're assuming that I have . . ."

Now he's the one raising the eyebrow.

"Well, obviously I have," I clarify. "At least I *think* I have. I mean I was out in the woods and everything. There were birds there—a robin, a cardinal, a crow. I'm not sure I could identify any of the others, but they were definitely birds. Definitely, definitely birds . . ."

I hear my explanation filtered through Steve's ears and figure he'll be wishing me well any second now.

But he doesn't. Rather than cut me loose, he walks me through my paces.

"You got binoculars?"

I tell him I'm borrowing a pair.

"What guide you got?"

For street cred purposes, I don't dare mention the bird app on my phone. (*Do real birders even use apps?* I wonder.) The truth is I've yet to settle upon a proper field guide. I've narrowed it down to a few, but I don't yet know if I'm smitten with Sibley's or partial to Peterson's, an uncertainty that I imagine will raise another red flag for Steve. At this moment in time, my allegiance falls mostly to a copy of the Golden Library of Knowledge's 1958 classic *Birds of the World*, a children's book, more or less. I'd retrieved my copy at a library book sale a few weeks prior, attracted by its assumption that the reader had no prior knowledge of the existence of birds, proof of which I'd gleaned by the perfunctory title on the opening page: "What Are Birds?"

Long story short, the book spoke to me.

Thankfully, bird identification hasn't changed too dramatically in the decades since the book's publication, though there have, of course, been modifications to habitat, migration patterns, not to mention that we've lost a few species along the way.

It's a troubling realization: that there were birds in the world my parents might've seen that I'll never see myself. Equally burdensome is lugging this line of thought into the future: that there are birds *I* might've seen that my children won't.

Writing of the Passenger Pigeon, in 1947 renowned Wisconsin conservationist Aldo Leopold came to a similarly disheartening conclusion.

"Men still live who, in their youth, remember pigeons; trees still live that, in their youth, were shaken by a living wind. But a few decades hence only the oldest oaks will remember, and at long last only the hills will know."

Of course, men like Leopold have been sounding this alarm for quite some time, the most recent sounding courtesy of the *State of the Birds* report, a collaborative study that, for the past five years, has drawn attention to the declining populations of avian species. The report lists the species most at risk, and though it isn't meant to function as a death list per se, I can't help but view it as an early draft.

In the 2014 report the authors piggyback on the one-hundred-year anniversary of the extinction of the Passenger Pigeon, describing how flocks "a billion-birds strong" once clouded the skies until those skies were cleared by pigeoners. These were men who knew how to turn pigeons into profits, and as a result of the unregulated market, they sold their birds by the barrel.

The report, too, incorporates the "from billions to one" language and, to put an even finer point on it, reminds us that the birds' decline occurred in "half a person's lifetime." The comparison is hardly subtle, forcing us to face yet another difficult environmental truth: that a single generation of humans in a single section of the planet could lift their guns, shoot blindly, and obliterate a species that had thrived prior to our encounters with it.

If there's a headline to be drawn from the 2014 report, it's that while conservation efforts appear to be working, we need more of them to reverse the course for birds in decline. As for the causes of decline, the report cites habitat loss first and foremost, though it goes on to note a few others ways in which humans affect bird populations directly. As I read on, I expect to receive a lecture on irresponsible hunting practices; how much in the same way hunters of the past decimated the Passenger Pigeon, hunters of the present now set their sights on other species, with equally disastrous results.

Not so, according to the report.

The real trouble, apparently, are house cats.

That's right, that saber-toothed creature currently batting a ball of yarn beside your feet is second only to habitat loss in causing bird populations to dwindle. Yet we can't blame cats alone. After all, we're the ones who allow them open hunting season 365 days a year.

Though not a current cat owner, I grew up with one, and throughout my childhood, rarely a week went by when Morris, our great tabby hunter, didn't bestow upon our doorstep one shredded bird or another. Who knows how much blood he had on his claws and, by extension, how much blood we had on our hands.

But the bloodshed doesn't stop with cats. While cats are estimated to kill approximately 2.4 billion birds per year throughout the United States, building windows remain a secondary threat, claiming an additional 600 million birds annually. To combat this scourge, several cities have adopted "best practices" for protecting birds from fatal window collisions, though the combination of glass treatment, external lightning, and carefully placed greenery has yet to eliminate the threat.

Inside the bird museum, there are no cats, no windows, no threats.

But also: not a single bird at risk.

As I once learned all too well, windows are far from the only structural threat that faces the modern bird.

One morning while drinking coffee with my wife, we paused midsip upon hearing a trilling coming from inside the wall. We lived in a World War II–era duplex then, and though we'd grown accustomed to a wide variety of noises coming from the walls (mostly cockroaches; this was graduate school), the trilling was a new one on us.

"What is it?" my wife whispered.

"I'm not sure," I said, "it almost sounds like a . . . bird."

It was the closest I could come to the truth—that it *was* a bird, undoubtedly, and that the bird was trapped in our wall.

Back then, I knew even less about birds than I do now, which meant for the twenty-four hours or so in which we inadvertently held that creature captive, I was forced to envision him (or her) as any number of species: a robin, a sparrow, a Blue Jay, an Ivory-bill, for all I knew.

Eventually my wife headed off to work, while I stayed home to write. By which I mean I spent the day trying to pinpoint the bird's exact location within the wall and, upon doing so, withdrew the hammer from the toolkit and dared myself to violate the lease. Our deposit was eight hundred dollars—*Surely enough to cover a bit of drywall,* I thought—but we were mostly broke back then, and that deposit was meant to serve as our next deposit, too.

Since I hadn't factored "unforeseeable bird-related expenses" into our threadbare budget, I held off on the hammering. Instead, I did the reasonable thing and called the landlord, who himself did the reasonable thing by entering our rental an hour or so later to provide an in-depth analysis of our situation.

"Yup," he concluded, tapping the wall twice, "sometimes birds get stuck in walls."

As I watched the landlord drive away, I knew I was that bird's last hope to do the next best reasonable thing.

I reached once more for the hammer, aiming the head toward the wall and urging myself to do it.

Though I didn't do it.

Eight hundred dollars, I decided, was too high a price for some bird I didn't even know by name.

The following day, once the trilling stopped, I convinced myself that the bird in the nearby tree was the bird that was once in our wall.

It made for a good story, at least, just the happily ever after I was after.

When eagles fall in love, Steve tells me, they fall in love. Literally.

Talons locked, the male and female grip one another in free fall, dropping from heaven to earth in what can only be described as some kind of Romeo-and-Juliet-inspired death cult. Or love cult. Or something in between.

It's known as cartwheeling, a kind of synchronized skydiving shared between monogamous birds.

On a good day, the eagles release talons in the final moments, triumphantly peeling back into the air. But on a bad day, they become living proof that love does not conquer all—especially gravity—putting into peril the happily ever after *they* were after.

Of course, when humans fall in love with a bird, the ritual is far less dramatic. There's no sky show, that's for sure, just a gaping-mouthed human peering through binoculars trying hard not to swallow a fly. But as many birders will tell you, spotting a sought-after bird is only half the fun, the other half coming by way of the story you get to tell afterward.

Steve explains this to me shortly after we leave the museum and take our seats alongside the fireplace in the nearby student center.

"Birds are amazing," he says at the conclusion of his eagle lecture. "But it's not just them. I mean, if you tell someone that a woodpecker's tongue originates in its nostril, wraps around its skull, goes under its skin, then back up through the bottom of its mouth so it can protract its barb-tipped tongue in order to slurp a bug like a tape measure, well," he says breathlessly, "that's pretty amazing, too, don't you think?"

I'm so wrapped up in the image of a tongue wrapped round a skull that I can barely nod my own.

Between the eagles and the woodpeckers, I'm already sold on Steve's "birds are amazing" argument, though he doesn't stop there. Instead, he dedicates another fifteen minutes or so to ticking off evolutionary fun facts.

"I mean, you could just tell people interesting things about birds till the end of time," he says.

You could, I think, peering out the window at what appears to be some kind of sparrow.

But as Steve makes clear, you needn't be an expert on birds to appreciate what they offer us. Sure, they're environmentally valuable and aesthetically pleasing, but beyond all that, they also give us a chance to spin our yarns with feathers.

New York Times reporter Jack Hitt first made their narrative qualities clear to me in a 2006 article on the Ivory-billed Woodpecker.

"Each bird is a tiny protagonist in a tale of natural history," Hitt wrote, "the story of a niche told in a vivid language of color, wing shape, body design, habitat, bill size, movement, flying style and perching habits. The more you know about each individual bird, the better you are at telling this tale."

As expected, Steve can tell a pretty good one.

"Tell me about your most memorable sighting," I say, "about your Holy Grail bird."

Even from behind his glasses, I can see his eyes glaze with nostalgia.

"It was back when I was down in South Carolina," he begins. "I guess it was 2004 or so . . ."

As Steve tells it, he was driving across a bridge one warm spring afternoon when a glance in the rearview revealed a glimpse of a bird bursting past.

"I thought, 'What the hell was that?'" Steve recounts, leaping from his chair. "So I slowed the car for a better look, and then I see them— they're Swallow-tailed Kites! I literally slam on the brakes and stop the car on the middle of the bridge. There's no one around, so I get out and I just watch the three of them sparring. The first two sort of fly out of view, but the last one," Steve says, jumping to his feet, "the last one reaches out and catches a dragonfly! It's all just one quick motion," he says, turning his hand into a claw and doing his best dragonfly-catching impersonation.

"Meanwhile, I'm doing one of these," he says, forming an *O* with his mouth and shifting his head toward the ceiling of the student center. "And then, all of the sudden, all three of the birds disappear over the trees."

"And that was that," I say.

"That was that," he agrees, collapsing into his chair with a faraway look on his face. "Birds . . . wow . . . have I told you they're amazing?"

Summers as a child I took to the woods: climbing trees, building forts, lifting rocks in search of bugs I'd never seen before. I'd leave shortly after breakfast, ambling home only when lunchtime demanded it. Afternoons I'd return to the wilderness; there was always work to be done—something to build, something to break, something to discover. The hours and days passed at hummingbird speed, all of them seemingly perfect.

As I grew older, my bug box and butterfly net began to gather a bit of dust in the closet. I can't explain why, though I imagine the hypnotic allure of video games had something to do with it. That I, like so many of my generation, traded scraped knees and muddy shoes for a pair of mushroom-eating plumbers, gave up bug bites and poison ivy, too, for a chance to hunt ducks with a plastic gun. By age ten, my days of outdoor exploration were already in decline, and I've struggled to reverse course ever since.

When I admit this to Steve—that nature and I have been growing apart for nearly two decades—he insists we give it another go, certain there's still some love between us.

"Come on now," he says, "you must have some natural curiosity left."

"Oh, I'm plenty curious," I say. "I just don't have any answers. And even if I was back out there every day putting beetles in bug boxes, I wouldn't be able to name a single one."

Steve nods. He's dealt with people like me before.

"When I give talks," he says, "I often do an experiment. I ask the people in the audience to give me two minutes of their time. 'For the first minute,' I say, 'name as many of these as you can: fashion designers, musical acts, sports team, actors, whatever—you pick your category.' Then, for the second minute, I ask them to name as many birds as they can."

"How bad is it?" I ask.

"On average," Steve says, "people can name about 7 birds. As for the other categories, they get around 21.5."

"Triple," I say, unable to hide my disappointment.

"People know what they know," Steve shrugs. "They know fashion or music or sports team or actors. But then they go outside and they can't name that tree over there," he says, pointing out the window. "They can't name the types of clouds in the sky. Can't even name a single constellation. People are just . . ."—he pauses for the right word—"oblivious. Since we don't know the names of things, we don't have a problem forgetting they exist."

He cites the *State of the Birds* report as proof.

"As of this year there are 314 climate-endangered or threatened birds. And it's because we're messing with their habitats, because we're not paying attention."

My mind leaps to our earlier conversation in the bird museum, when Steve had seemed far less concerned over the fate of the thought-to-be-extinct Bachman's Warbler.

I call him on it, ask why he'd been so casual in writing off that particular species given his great care for birds generally.

"Well, they haven't been seen in over forty years," he reminds me.

"Right, but I guess . . . I wonder if you have an emotional response to that. About losing birds in your lifetime."

"I'm sad as hell," Steve says, equally matter-of-fact. "And the Bachman's just one more to be sad about. All the reports are now showing transference of ranges. You take a Bald Eagle or a Common Loon, for instance, by the end of the century, they won't be in Wisconsin anymore. Now, if you don't know those birds even exist you won't miss them, but if you do know . . . if you know their names, and if you're fond of them . . ."

As he trails off, I peer out the window at a tree I cannot name.

"You have a responsibility," Steve says gently. "And I've said this to my own kids, too. We all have to justify our existence, to ask ourselves what we plan to do with our time here. Are we going to give something back to our fellow humans? The world? Because if we *can't* justify our time here, then what is the point of life?"

My eyes refuse to leave the tree outside the window.

"Look," he says, adjusting to meet my gaze, "maybe not everyone will know the name of that tree. But maybe they'll at least take the time to acknowledge that the tree is photosynthetic, and that it grows here in Wisconsin. That it has a place, a need, a role. And maybe just knowing that will help people realize how all things are connected."

The problem, Steve explains, isn't just our obliviousness, but our refusal to combat our obliviousness until the sky begins to fall, or rather, until things begin falling from it.

"The Passenger Pigeon is a classic example," Steve says. "It wasn't until after we'd already killed all of them that people started thinking, 'Huh, I guess we *can* cause extinction.' That's when the conservation movement really started; once we realized we could wipe out an entire population of birds without even really trying."

Steve pauses, his eyes retaining the same faraway look he'd mustered for his Swallow-tailed story.

I glance at my watch to learn it's nearly class time, so I rise to my feet.

"Listen," I say, "I learned a lot today. Thank you."

This time Steve is the one snapped back to reality. He nods, smiles, says we should do it again sometime, that there's plenty more to learn.

As I step outside, the warm October breeze cuts through the tree whose name I still don't know.

I stare at its branches, allowing my mind to drift to the memory of a bird once stuck in my wall.

Had I known her name, I wonder, *might I have set her free?*

3

The Hermit and the Hawk

You are right that the only foolish animal is the "man." Perhaps he would be less so
if he would realize that he is an animal.
—Francis Zirrer in a letter to A. W. "Bill" Schorger, 1942

The hermit had a name but no one knew it, or almost no one did.
Francis Zirrer preferred it that way.

What was the use of being known, after all, if one might remain
otherwise?

According to the 1920 census, Zirrer immigrated to America in 1912,
though what remains less clear is from where he was coming. The census
indicates that he was born in Carnolia (what today we call Slovenia)
but offers little on the specifics of his locale prior to immigration. From
somewhere in southeastern Europe, no doubt, but I can't pin down a
place with certainty. What we do know is that following his arrival in
America, he spent much of the next half century in the wilds of Wisconsin, taking refuge alongside his invalid wife, Clara, in a cabin far
from society's prying eyes. Their remote location provided unfettered

access to nature's grand displays, many of which Zirrer recorded with great poeticism. Such as the return of the bitterns in the springtime, their "ghostly forms" croaking through the night; and the ravens, too, whose wing beats hummed like "an approaching storm" long before he ever saw them.

Yet for all his observations of the natural world, Zirrer left few clues about himself behind. In fact, most of what we know of him we owe to Passenger Pigeon expert and Wisconsin conservationist A. W. "Bill" Schorger. Between 1934 and 1949 the pair exchanged letters on a range of topics: ice-gnawing muskrats, tunneling minks, the ripening of hazelnuts. No observation was too small for the curious men, and over time, as their correspondence grew, so too did Zirrer's paper trail.

While not all the letters survived, a great many have, providing insight into the conservation concerns shared between two mid-twentieth-century Wisconsinites. In some respects they could not be more different (Schorger served as city mouse to Zirrer's country mouse), though their shared affection for nature allowed their seemingly unconventional relationship to flourish.

If you've never heard of Francis Zirrer, you're in good company. Had I not stumbled across his letters to Schorger, he would still be a stranger to me. Upon reading them, I immediately become aware of Zirrer's talent as a nature writer, though after a bit more research, am disappointed to learn that his body of published work is limited to eight or so articles in the Wisconsin Society for Ornithology's publication, the *Passenger Pigeon*, as well as a handful of newspaper articles. Beyond these written contributions, he's most remembered (assuming he's remembered at all) for confirming the Northern Goshawks' nesting in Wisconsin—plenty more on that story later.

Though initially, of most interest to me is the man himself—a nature-loving recluse whose decision to "opt out" of the modern world afforded him insight into the natural one.

How does someone do it? I wonder as I sift through his letters. *How does one simply wave goodbye?*

In today's world, perhaps Zirrer's choice is akin to clinging to a flip phone rather than conforming to the smart phone revolution. It's a decision I admire, even if I—a twitchy, focus-fractured member of the twenty-first century—can't quite commit to it myself. I have little doubt I would be much happier less connected, though I've fallen victim to the burdens of connectivity. After all, there are always emails to be emailed, tweets to be tweeted, and statuses in need of constant updating. Zirrer chose otherwise; he cut connections and took to the woods, instead.

As a result, scholarship on Zirrer's life is nearly as rare as the man was. In fact, it's mostly limited to the work of a single person, Wisconsin Department of Natural Resources conservation biologist Sumner Matteson. His three-part article on Zirrer's life in the woods offered me insight beyond the letters, helping me to understand the man within the context of his time. In his work, Matteson notes that Zirrer may "potentially" be one of Wisconsin's greatest naturalists, albeit one of its most unknown. Which is perhaps as Zirrer would've wanted it—a legacy as far removed from the spotlight as he.

While men like Zirrer were indeed rare, he was far from the only rarity to inhabit Wisconsin's wilderness. In a letter dated November 6, 1934, Zirrer confirmed that Schorger was likely correct that the Canada Jay was "practically extinct as a Wisconsin bird."

"It probably never was very abundant here," Zirrer lamented, "a bird of coniferous region had to go like so many others, when its original haunts were destroyed."

Habitat loss became a common theme throughout Zirrer's letters, likely because it affected not only the animals, but also Zirrer's encounters alongside them.

Fifteen years later, as Zirrer and Schorger's correspondence neared its end, the hermit echoed his concern for natural habitats.

"This locality used to be very good," he wrote of the forest surrounding his Hayward home. "But during the last few years most of the saleable trees [have] been cut down," he continued, "leaving only the young, the useless, the dead and the dying ones."

He added that this human-induced destruction (see also: Ivory-billed Woodpecker) had diminished the region's biodiversity as well.

"Over wide areas the flora [has] greatly changed," he wrote, "and many of the choicest plants completely gone."

It was an observation that might have gone unnoticed by the occasional outdoorsman, but Zirrer was anything but. For him, a tree was never just a tree; it was a tamarack, or a white spruce, or a balsam fir. His knack for learning the names of things would've swelled Steve Betchkal's heart, though Zirrer's motive for doing so was simply an outgrowth of living his life as an amateur field biologist. For the always-curious Zirrer, every walk in the woods was a fact-finding mission, another chance to reveal one of nature's great mysteries.

A city mouse myself, it's easy for me to envy this seemingly sylvan lifestyle, what on the surface seems like an existence of sun-dappled morning strolls through the foliage coupled with afternoon naps beneath trees. Though, of course, the life of a twentieth-century hermit was far more difficult than my rose-colored interpretation. There was always wood to be chopped, fires to be stoked, and vegetables to be gathered, just to name a few of the daily chores.

As I read their letters, I can't help but wonder if Bill Schorger was equally envious of Zirrer's "unencumbered" life; if he, too, preferred the flip phone lifestyle over the smart phone alternative.

Did Schorger ever want to escape the indignities of modern living, I wonder, *to leave behind his job as the president of a company and, later, a professor of wildlife management, and take to the woods, instead?*

It's possible, though perhaps it was Schorger's rootedness and Zirrer's freedom that allowed the partnership to thrive, a symbiotic relationship in which each man had something to offer the other. While Schorger undoubtedly provided Zirrer a foothold in the scientific world, Zirrer provided Schorger a foothold in the natural one. From warblers to woodpeckers, Zirrer documented every last creature he could, not only for his personal interest, but also in the hope that his observations might interest his friend.

Yet every nuthatch and Ruffed Grouse would serve as prologue for Zirrer's most lasting contribution—the discovery of Wisconsin's goshawk, the bird that, for better or worse, would forever alter Zirrer's relationship with the wild.

My own first goshawk sighting occurs eighty or so years after Zirrer's. And when I see it, it isn't even alive, but one of James Newman Clark's taxidermied specimens on display in the dead bird museum. It's positioned between the owls and the parrots, its sharp beak pointed menacingly toward me, its red eye daring me to move.

Even stuffed, I recognize the goshawk's regality. Measuring in at nearly two feet tall, its sharp claws lead me to believe it could probably pluck an entire colony of ice-gnawing muskrats without having to ruffle too many feathers. The bird, after all, is notorious for its hunting acumen, a skill that's been honed for hundreds of years throughout the world. Since the thirteenth century, the Japanese noble and samurai classes have trained this species to hunt an array of animals, including cranes, despite their David-versus-Goliath size differential. Unlike other predatory birds, the goshawk does not strike its prey, but clings to it, driving the unfortunate creature to the ground before killing it. It is a method, Zirrer would learn, that the brazen birds would try on humans, too.

According to his letters, Zirrer allegedly spotted his first goshawk in 1933, though initially he remained mum on his finding. While the hermit knew his sighting would surely be of great interest to the birding community, he also knew he'd risk his solitude by making the sighting public. Yet when the birds returned in the spring of 1934, Zirrer couldn't help but share the news with Owen Gromme, a curator at the Milwaukee Public Museum, as well as the author and artist of the highly acclaimed illustrated guide *Birds of Wisconsin*. An early conservationist, Gromme's interest was indeed sparked by Zirrer's goshawk claim; so much so that on May 16, 1934, he and his assistant Walter Pelzer completed the three-hundred-mile journey from Milwaukee to Zirrer's Rusk County cabin.

In his previous day's field notes, Gromme noted that though they had yet to meet, his brief correspondence with Zirrer had persuaded him that he was a "man of some scientific knowledge," as well as "a confirmed conservationist." Later Gromme would write how "gratifying" it was to meet a man like Zirrer, "whose sympathies were with, instead of against the Hawks and who guarded their secret jealously." Though some, including Zirrer, might argue that he hadn't, in fact, guarded their secret jealously enough.

As the museum men entered the property, Zirrer attempted hospitality. But it was perhaps a challenge given his general distrust of people, particularly people whom he feared might collect a goshawk specimen for their museum regardless of his preference that they not. This potential difference of opinion was in many ways a microcosm of the era's shifting views on ornithological study. While many ornithologists and birders still preferred guns to field glasses, as a result of the rise of field guides, the shoot-now-look-later approach had begun to fall out of favor. And for the nature-loving Zirrer, the goshawks were far better use to him roosting in a nearby tree then stuffed and placed on exhibit across the state.

Which leaves me to wonder why he felt compelled to share the goshawk's secret in the first place. Was he trying to impress the curator in an attempt to gain greater inclusion within the scientific community? And if so, was a goshawk the price of admission?

Upon Gromme and Pelzer's arrival, Zirrer guided the men to a yellow birch tree adjacent to the nest. As the men assembled their photographic blind, Gromme realized that the branches in the nesting tree obscured their view. Gromme—who perhaps knew better than to take the risk himself—encouraged Pelzer to climb the nesting tree to clear the branches. Pelzer agreed, though he'd barely begun shimmying up the bough before being attacked by the female goshawk.

Though the tree's branches obscured the nest, nothing obscured the action that followed. In his later writings on this moment, Gromme described "the vigorous strokes" of the mother bird's "powerful wings" and how she "gave her victim a thump on the back that could be heard from some distance."

Had Pelzer "not been held to the tree by the strong leather belt," Gromme wrote, "he most certainly would have been knocked from it." To Pelzer's credit, the faithful assistant completed his mission and, upon returning to solid ground, was greeted by Gromme and Zirrer, the latter of whom noted that Pelzer "looked with a mixture of sadness and amusement at his shirt, which was hanging in tatters."

Returning to the blind the following week, Gromme endured a similarly brutal attack—making it halfway up the bough before the bird resumed her assault. The pair sparred in the air, Gromme's swing-and-a-miss soon countered by the goshawk's direct blow to the intruder's head. She drew blood, prompting Gromme to hastily descend the tree, then retreat to a nearby stream to clean his wound.

"From that time on," Gromme reported, "all ascents to either tree were made with the head well protected by heavy burlap or a sheepskin-lined leather helmet."

The goshawk's message was clear: no one messes with mama.

While the attacks were well documented by both Gromme and Zirrer, what remains unclear is how Zirrer reacted to the museum men's pummeling.

Who, I wonder eighty years later, *was he rooting for?*

Just days after reading Zirrer's letters, I too find myself picking sides.

At around 9:00 p.m. on a Tuesday night, as I sift through my "needs-to-be-graded" pile of literature papers, I'm interrupted by a hoot.

Specifically, a: *hoo, hoo, hoo, hoooo, hoooo . . .*

It's no goshawk, I know that much.

Reaching for my phone, I scroll through my Audubon app until I arrive at the owls.

Barred or Great Horned? I wonder, swiping between their photos.

I pull the screen door wide, stand shivering in my t-shirt/long johns combo as the single-digit temperatures seize upon me.

Teeth chattering, I linger in the shadows, anxious for my owl to return.

And then:

Hoo, hoo, hoo, hoooo, hoooo . . .

My gaze shifts to the silhouettes of my backyard pines refracting off the snow. Then, back to the Audubon app as I replay a recorded hoot that syncs perfectly with what I now know to be a pair of Great Horned Owls skulking in the trees.

I slip back inside the house to rouse my two-and-a-half-year-old son, Henry, from the clutches of near sleep.

"Hey boy," I whisper. "Wanna hear some owls?"

"Hmm?"

"Owls. You know, like in *Winnie-the-Pooh*?"

Now I'm speaking his language, and though my wife—who lies beside him—is less than thrilled by my impetuous breech of the sleep routine, she can hear the excitement in my voice.

"Let's go find him," Henry agrees—anything to stave off bedtime.

He crawls to the edge of the bed, then pitter-patters down the darkened hall.

I give chase, and within moments, we return to the screen door. Responsible parent that I am, this time we opt to stay inside, though our screen barrier does little to keep out the cold.

"Where is him?" Henry whispers, his eyes locked on the trees.

"Well, if I had to guess I'd say . . ."

Hoo, hoo, hoo, hoooo, hoooo . . .

Henry gasps, turns toward me, then offers his reply.

"Hoochey boo!" he calls. "Hookie doo!"

His unexpected interruption silences even the owls, who now wonder what unknown creature *they're* dealing with.

And then, the cause of their hooting reveals itself:

"Rabbit!" Henry hollers, his finger darting like a divination rod.

Where did he learn about rabbits? I wonder.

And then it hits me: *Winnie-the-Pooh.*

Uh-oh. If this goes bad, I think, *this kid's going to have a complicated understanding of the realities of the food chain in the Hundred Acre Wood . . .*

Nevertheless, I don't shield him from the show. Instead, we watch that rabbit's death-defying run with our eyes wide, marveling at the way he slaloms through the snow, half transformed to apparition. I hold my breath, praying to God our rabbit might live to die another day, preferably someday when we're not there to serve as witnesses.

I make no secret of the team I'm rooting for—"Run, rabbit, run!"—and soon Henry joins the chant.

Our interjections seem only to further incite the owls' bloodlust, and as the hooting intensifies, I brace myself for the inevitable strike, for the flash of wings followed by the scream.

But there is no scream. Not yet.

Instead, the rabbit makes a sharp right around the corner of the house, exploding through the frozen leaves before taking refuge beneath our minivan parked in the drive.

Henry and I follow the action as best we can, me carrying him football-style beneath my arm as he Supermans toward the front window.

From our place at the window, I swear I can see every last twitch of that rabbit's nose as he trembles beside the back tire. And then, as the owls take their positions on the nearby branches, he makes his final run—a fear-induced sprint across the icy street to the safety of the neighbor's yard.

Every moment is captured beneath the glow of the streetlight, his shadow scurrying alongside him like a decoy.

Hoo, hoo, hoo, hoooo, hoooo . . .

Followed by:

Hoo, hoo, hoo, hoooo, hoooo . . .

Followed by:

Silence.

The show is over, anticlimax has won, the rabbit vanishes beneath a bush.

"What happened to him?" Henry asks, his eyes as wide as the owls'.

I am breathless, heart racing.

"Nothing," I say, carrying him back to bed. "Nothing happened to him tonight."

We've all heard the expression: a bird in the hand is worth two in the bush. Yet I imagine Zirrer would've preferred the latter option, well aware that a man with a bird in his hand generally meant that bird was dead.

While Zirrer may have had some initial concerns about the museum men's potential interest in obtaining a specimen, he soon realized that the true threat to the goshawks came from beyond the scientific community.

In a 1935 letter to Schorger, Zirrer urged his friend to remain mum on the goshawks' location.

"I have plenty of reasons for being careful," he explained cryptically.

In a follow-up letter he clarified his comment, noting how during Gromme and Pelzer's visit the previous year, the men had no choice but to take into their confidence the property owner on whose land the birds had nested.

"Consequently the birds were much advertised and bragged about," Zirrer wrote, "partially due also to the desire of making some money out of it."

By outing the birds as he had, Zirrer feared he'd inadvertently put a price tag on their feathered backs, particularly for his quick-on-the-trigger neighbors. Arthur Allen and his wife had made the same miscalculation a decade prior—drawing attention to the Ivory-bill pair in the Florida swamp, which ultimately led to the pair's demise.

Both stories have their ironic twist, though Zirrer's story serves as a morality tale as well: for a man who valued his privacy so deeply, in this instance, he had little regard for the privacy of his feathered guests in the trees. The rare birds had graced him with their presence, and in return, Zirrer had made their presence known to men. In his defense, he'd mostly offered information on the goshawks only on a need-to-know basis; the trouble, though, was that the property owner needed to know.

In an effort to return the goshawks to their anonymity, in the spring of 1935 Zirrer retrieved a long pole and knocked the nest from its perch, hoping that the birds might retreat deeper into the woods and farther from humankind's intrusions.

His efforts failed to persuade.

"The hawks had begun to build another nest," he confessed to Schorger, "not more than sixty to eighty yards from the old one."

Zirrer's moral crisis is not without precedent, at least in the literary world.

In tenth-grade English I was assigned to read Sarah Orne Jewett's canonical "The White Heron," a story starring a nine-year-old girl named Sylvie who must decide whether to reveal the location of a pair of herons to an ornithologist in search of the birds. It makes for a difficult dilemma, one in which Sylvie must decide whether her allegiance is to animal or man. Her decision is complicated further by the ornithologist's dashing good looks—which, in Sylvie's rural wilderness, made him a specimen as sought after as the herons themselves.

When Sylvie's grandmother asks the ornithologist if he cages his birds, he replies, "Oh, no, they're stuffed and preserved, dozens and dozens of them."

It's enough to give Sylvie pause, to make her question if her desire to please the young man is worth condemning the birds to death.

The next day, Sylvie follows the ornithologist into the woods—following, but never leading. Throughout the day he shows her many kindnesses: teaching her about birds, pointing out live ones, even giving her a jackknife as a gift.

"[Sylvie] had never seen anyone so charming and delightful," the narrator notes. "The woman's heart, asleep in the child, was vaguely thrilled by a dream of love."

In the story's final pages, Sylvie climbs a white pine—"the last of its generation"—until she comes face-to-face with the male heron. Upon spotting her, the male issues a warning cry to his mate roosting in the nearby nest, an encounter so magical that by the time Sylvie descends back to earth, her lips are locked tight.

She cannot do it, the narrator confirms, cannot "tell the heron's secret and give its life away."

Nearly half a century after the story's publication, Zirrer and the goshawk offer the alternative ending: the one where man's lips are unlocked, the secret spilled, and all happily-ever-afters relegated to fiction.

In a letter dated September 26, 1943—after three typewritten pages dedicated to the usual subjects (Arctic Three-toed Woodpeckers, flying squirrels, among other species observed in his backyard bog)—Zirrer added a handwritten note about his own waning happiness.

"This letter would have been written sooner, but since the 28 of

August we struggle with death. My wife is very seriously ill. It is just this week that there is a slight improvement noticeable. Personally I have not had much sleep since."

Over the coming months Clara Zirrer's condition would worsen, an illness that ultimately led to her death in a Milwaukee hospital in 1944.

For over a year, Schorger and Zirrer's correspondence reached a near standstill, and in September 1946, when Zirrer at last returned to the typewriter with some regularity, he seemed a different man.

In a letter from May 1945, Zirrer hinted toward a reason for his drop-off in communication.

"Since the death of my wife," he began, "the finest and grandest woman that had ever been born, or lived, in U.S. or for that matter anywhere else, . . . I have done very little field work: there is not the interest the way it used to be. No man had ever had a better companion, a truer friend than I in my, though invalid wife—invalid for over 25 years."

Matteson speculates that Zirrer's diminished enthusiasm for the natural world was directly linked to Clara's death.

"Perhaps Zirrer had served as his wife's eyes and ears, describing his observations to her in detail before committing them to letters," Matteson speculates. "Without her presence, her companionship, his interest faded."

Whatever the cause, his interest faded rapidly.

Mere paragraphs after confiding his grief, Zirrer pushed himself to return to his usual, nature-observing self; though his observations, too, seemed laced with loneliness.

"The owls cavity is still empty," Zirrer informed Schorger, "and I have, all winter, not heard a sound indicating that they are here."

After a few failed stints in various cities (first Milwaukee, then Chicago), Zirrer retreated once more into the wilderness, dedicating much of his final years to the landscape he knew best. In his last published work—a 1959 article for the *Milwaukee Journal*—Zirrer described his most recent winter in the woods. Titled "Nature Lover's North Woods Diary," the article shared the seventy-three-year-old's insight into a world few of the newspaper's readers could understand.

"The cabin ... was the home of several deer mice—cute little beasties, glossy tawny brown above and snowy white under," Zirrer began. "They ran up and down the walls and beams better than a squirrel. Last fall, after noticing these squatters, I bought a few traps but decided not to use them."

Grateful for the companionship, Zirrer fed them daily, eventually earning their trust.

"Now," he wrote, "[the mice] come, one after another, pick a piece of food, sit on their haunches like diminutive squirrels and, transferring the food from their mouths to their tiny, handlike paws, start to eat daintily. If there is more than they can eat at one sitting, they carry it away and hide it," he explained, "sometimes in my boots."

Though some readers may have taken Zirrer's band of merry mice as proof of a man who'd lost his marbles, others surely admired the provincial life he'd established. Yet his animal visitors could hardly replace his wife, and as the years wore on, the fine line between self-imposed solitude and loneliness appeared to be wavering toward the latter.

In what would become his swan song, Zirrer dedicated his final published words to a familiar theme: the destruction of the natural world.

"Outside my cabin the forest looks empty and desolate," he wrote. "Before long, however, the chain saws will be back here. In spite of conservation talk, the woods are still exploited to the limit. Every tree that is not too small must go. There is hardly a day that I don't hear the distant buzzing of the chainsaw."

Upon reading the line, my mind returns immediately to Don Eckelberry, whose two-week stint in the Singer Tract in 1944 had proved equally haunting. Not only was Eckelberry burdened with sketching what was believed to be the last American Ivory-billed Woodpecker, but he was forced to do so while the hum of the donkey engine served as a less than subtle reminder of the habitat disappearing around him.

I imagine Zirrer felt equally melancholic about his own diminished habitat. For a man who'd claimed a front-row seat to nature's grand display, as the curtain closed, he could barely stand to watch what little was left of it. Gone were the days of the grackles and the Audubon Warblers. Gone, too, were the moonless nights spent peering at the bladderwort and the leather-leaf that covered his sedge-filled bog.

The call of the goshawk had long ago been replaced by the shrill cry of the chainsaw, and when he could stand it no more, he left his home one last time, retreating into death in the same Milwaukee hospital where his wife had died twenty-four years prior.

What are we to make of a man like Francis Zirrer? A man so dead-set against being known that it only makes me want to know him more.

After several siftings through the few clues at my disposal, I realize that Francis Zirrer is, to some extent, a man I've concocted in my head. He was real, of course, though the motives I've thrust upon him are based mostly on the letters left behind. I'm desperate for further interpretations, though when it comes to Francis Zirrer few are offered. Yet this lack of information hardly keeps me from wondering if men like Zirrer still exist, if their opt-out lifestyle is still possible in the modern world.

For an answer, I call up sixty-two-year-old Sumner Matteson, my port in the storm on all things Zirrer related. Though we've never met in person, after a few minutes of chatter, Sumner and I immediately connect over our shared interest in a man so few remember.

"Are people like Zirrer still out there?" I ask. "People who still live in such seclusion?"

"There are certainly people still like him living here in Wisconsin," Sumner confirms without hesitation. "They're still out there, and that's what's so unique about Wisconsin, historically speaking. We have a way of producing these voices for our state, these voices for natural history. Only a few people may know them, but for those who do, they're very valued. This was certainly true of Zirrer."

I find myself nodding into the phone as Sumner preaches to our very small choir.

Admittedly, I'm no Zirrer, but that doesn't mean some part of me doesn't aspire to be. This becomes especially true on the days when my "needs-to-be-graded" pile of papers reaches sequoia heights. What I wouldn't give on those days to be the man in the bog in the nighttime, the one who, in early spring, lifts his head skyward, an ear cocked for the squall of the goshawk.

Despite the solace nature often afforded him, man rarely offered Zirrer such comfort.

In the midst of World War II, Zirrer penned a particularly pessimistic letter to Schorger, one that put his own species in the crosshairs.

"You are right," he wrote, "that the only foolish animal is the 'man.' Perhaps he would be less so if he would realize that he is an animal."

To this day, Zirrer's call for humility rings true. And though we are indeed animals, we are complicated further by our roles as predator, prey, and noncombatant. Zirrer witnessed these roles playing out throughout his lifetime, including one fall night in 1932 when, after waving goodbye to Clara, he struck off into the woods.

"It was a pleasant moonlit night," Zirrer recalled decades later, "and the pretty woodland creatures were frolicking."

Overhead an abundance of flying squirrels cascaded through the air, eventually "parachuting" upon his cabin's roof.

For the moment all was peaceful, but the moment would not last.

Out of the corner of his eye, Zirrer spotted a shadowy shape perched in a nearby spruce. Meanwhile, the squirrels, unaware of the threat, continued their rooftop acrobatics.

And then the shape took flight, Zirrer watching silently as the drama unfolded before him.

"When I realized that it was that fierce, grim 'flying terror of the night,' the Great Horned Owl, I was actually stunned," Zirrer wrote. "I did not know what to do. My first thought was to help, to save one of the lovely little creatures from death; but years of necessary caution exercised in observing wildlife restrained the impulse to move, to shout, to pick up and throw a stick at the owl."

Instead, he simply watched as the drama came to its close—the owl snagging its prey while the unlucky squirrel released an "agonizingly shrill, broken, gasping shriek."

As the wilderness returned to silence, Zirrer could just make out the squirrel's silhouette swinging from the owl's talons.

Zirrer had witnessed what Henry and I hadn't—a predator's capture of prey.

Later, he'd offer reflections on another owl's successful hunt, the latter example even more closely aligned with my own backyard observations.

Of a rabbit's owl-induced death, Zirrer wrote, "Of course I was sorry for the rabbit, but notwithstanding my sympathies I do not like to interfere with nature's order."

Not anymore, I thought, *given what he'd learned from the goshawk.*

PART II
Spotting

4

The Continuing Saga of the
Resurrection of the Lord God Bird

In a way, the bird means more as an idea than it ever could as a reality.
—Don Moser, "The Last Ivory Bill," 1972

When in search of an Ivory-billed Woodpecker, begin in the old forests and the cypress swamps where the poisonous creatures live. Then, keep your eyes glued to the trees, your binoculars glued to your eyes, and wait for the rare bird to appear.

Or do none of these things intentionally and still end up with a sighting.

Which is how it happened for Gene Sparling on February 11, 2004, as he kayaked the Cache River near Brinkley, Arkansas.

Sparling had been cruising for a while when he glanced up from paddling to glimpse a bird no longer thought to exist.

"When I did discuss (the sighting) I made no claims," Sparling is quoted in a 2005 issue of *BirdWatching* magazine. "I wouldn't want to be lumped in with the alien abduction hunters and Sasquatch stories.

I knew the legend of the Ivory-bill, and I knew it was extinct and had been my whole life."

Aware of the potential for catching flack, he nevertheless felt compelled to post a description of what he'd seen on a canoe club message board. Word virtually traveled from Hot Springs, Arkansas, to Ithaca, New York, where it prompted the attention of Tim Gallagher of the Cornell Lab of Ornithology.

Gallagher, an expert on the Ivory-bill—who at the time was writing a book on the subject—found credibility in Sparling's claim. He enlisted the help of his longtime birding buddy, an Alabama photography professor named Bobby Harrison, and together the pair teamed up with Sparling to continue to search the Cache.

At around lunchtime on February 27—the second day of the expedition—Gallagher and Harrison were paddling along when they, too, spotted what they believed to be an Ivory-bill darting across the bayou toward a nearby tupelo tree.

"Look at all the white on its wings!" Gallagher cried, and Harrison did, confirming the feature that most distinguished the Ivory-bill from its commonplace cousin, the Pileated Woodpecker.

The pair compared notes, and after corroborating their individual stories, Gallagher called home to report the news to his wife, journalist Rachel Dickinson.

"Had I known then that I was going to have to keep the biggest conservation secret of the past century to myself for almost 14 months," Dickinson wrote in a piece for *Audubon*, "I might have asked him not to divulge any of the details."

What happened next seemed more fitting for a Hollywood thriller than a scientific birding expedition.

Calls were made, important people were brought "into the know," and within weeks the New York–based Cornell Lab had partnered with a local chapter of the Nature Conservancy to begin work on the vaguely named "Arkansas Inventory Project," whose secret mission it was to find further evidence of the bird's reemergence.

For fourteen months a tight-lipped group of scientists and researchers continued their quest, until the spring of 2005, when the U.S.

Department of the Interior hosted a press conference to announce their findings.

As the cameras rolled, Cornell Lab director Dr. John Fitzpatrick took to the microphone, making clear both the cultural and scientific importance of finding a living Ivory-billed Woodpecker.

"This is no ordinary bird to the 70 million Americans who are bird watchers," he explained. "This Holy Grail is really the most spectacular creature we could imagine rediscovering."

At the press conference, U.S. Interior Secretary Gale Norton and Agriculture Secretary Mike Johanns announced a "multi-year, multi-million-dollar partnership" to "aid the rare bird's survival."

Scientists and ornithologists cheered the good news—even if, for some, the rare bird's return seemed unlikely.

Although it was hardly an Ivory-bill, my family encountered a rare bird of its own in the summer of 2004—well, rare to Fort Wayne, Indiana, at least. I'd recently completed my first year of college, and my parents—tired of their near-empty nest without me—did the logical thing and purchased an African Grey Parrot.

Long story short, if they were trying to fill the void I was leaving behind, they did so with relative ease.

It was my father's bird mostly. He was in the midst of a midlife crisis then, and since my mother wouldn't allow him a Harley-Davidson motorcycle ("Too dangerous," she'd argued) he bought a bird and named him after one.

Harley—the bird in question—was a mostly unlikable creature. Nobody could blame him. My parents had purchased him from a man who wanted to travel, which meant Harley, too, had to go.

For my father, the opportunity seemed too good to pass up: a parrot at a bargain price in desperate need of a home. He didn't think; he just bought him. Though Harley was still in his infancy (year one in a lifespan that often transcends half a century), his bond with his first owner had apparently already taken hold.

Either that, or he just hated us on principle.

In the best of times, Harley tolerated my father, and in the worst of times, he drew blood. Still, my father seemed up for the challenge, and in an effort to make that bird feel a little less lonely, that first summer I regularly witnessed Dad playing YouTube clips of Harley's feathered brethren for his bird. I can still see my father's shoulder-slumped silhouette as he and Harley stared at the screen, the way Dad tensed—at least initially—beneath the prick of Harley's claws. I remember, too, the way that bird was always vying for better positioning, constantly sidling from my father's arm toward his head, anxious to hold the higher ground.

Away at college for most of their relationship, I returned home that second Christmas to find Harley trapped in what I later learned was depression's icy embrace. A mere undergraduate with no formal training as a vet or a therapist, I'd failed to note the warning signs. Weight loss, withdrawal, and irritability all just seemed like character traits for Harley.

But it was more than that. Much more.

While my family and I spiraled lights around the Christmas tree, that bird of ours devised his terrible plan.

Meanwhile, back in Ithaca, what would become known as the Ivory-billed Woodpecker Recovery Team began making plans of their own.

For five seasons, Cornell's Ron Rohrbaugh served as the team's project director. On the Cornell Lab of Ornithology's *All About Birds* webpage dedicated to the search, Rohrbaugh reflected fondly on that first search season, describing the "electric" atmosphere that permeated throughout the team. Each ring of the cell phone had the potential to bring good news, Rohrbaugh recalled, though ultimately, the cell phone wouldn't ring nearly enough.

"In the first phase of the search," Rohrbaugh remembered, "we were all crammed into motel rooms, sleeping two to three to a room, eating out every night because we didn't have any kitchen facilities. We'd be out in the field from dawn until dusk every day, then come home and strip out of our wet clothes, throw on some dry ones, go grab a bite to eat, and then have a nighttime meeting."

Yet as the years dragged on and funding dried up, so too did the enthusiasm. In the annual reports, Rohrbaugh and his coauthors had no choice but to describe what little they'd discovered, the death knell appearing in the 2009 report, in which he and coauthors not only conceded that no Ivory-bills were seen, but also that no Ivory-bill calls or cavities were heard or spotted either.

The unbridled optimism of 2005 had all but been extinguished by 2010. After several unsuccessful expeditions, Rohrbaugh told *Discovery News* that even he thought it unlikely that there were "recoverable populations of ivory-billed woodpeckers in those places that have received significant search efforts over the past five years."

However, he added, moments later, "We haven't searched every place."

Indeed they hadn't, though Rohrbaugh's statement did little to persuade the doubters—and there were many of them.

As a result of what some viewed as a waste of money brought on by shoddy science, more than a few reputations were called into question. Yet perhaps the reputation that took the biggest hit belonged not to a person, but to an organization—the Cornell Lab of Ornithology, which had arguably done more for birding than any academic community in the country. Not only that, but it had served as the academic home for both Arthur Allen and James Tanner—the twentieth century's foremost Ivory-bill scholars.

One after another, even the most hopeful scientists began to concede that the story seemed a little too good to be true.

But what a wonderful storyline it would have made: how, against all odds, Cornell's next generation of Ivory-bill scholars completed the conservation work of their forbearers.

It wasn't to be.

By 2010, more than a few critics claimed that the Cornell Lab had egg on its face.

And it was not Ivory-bill egg.

In their defense, the scientists and ornithologists involved in the search believed what they believed for good reason. In the June 2005 issue of *Science*, Dr. John Fitzpatrick—along with sixteen coauthors—outlined the evidence in support of the bird's reemergence. As its centerpiece: a blurry, four-second clip of an alleged Ivory-bill in flight courtesy of David Luneau.

Luneau, a professor of electronics and computer engineering technology at the University of Arkansas at Little Rock, captured the footage on April 25, 2004, while canoeing the Bayou DeView in the Cache River. A member of the search team, he'd equipped his canoe with a continuously running video camera, thereby ensuring that any potential sighting might be captured on film. While the report acknowledges that the clip is indeed "blurred and pixilated," the authors nevertheless claimed it was proof enough of the bird's continued existence.

Not everyone shared the assessment.

In March 2006, David Sibley of *Sibley's Bird Guide* fame coauthored a counterpoint.

"We conclude that one cannot reject the hypothesis that the bird is a normal pileated woodpecker (i.e., the null expectation); moreover, the evidence firmly supports this hypothesis. Ivory-billed woodpeckers may persist in the southern United States, and we believe that conservation efforts on their behalf should continue. Verifiable evidence for the ivory-billed Woodpecker's persistence, however, is lacking."

Others, such as biologist Jerome Jackson, were more pointed in their criticism.

In the January 2006 issue of the *Auk*, a quarterly published by the American Ornithologists' Union, Jackson accused the article's authors of practicing "'faith based' ornithology," of making too much of too little.

For Jackson, it was a simple case of misidentification.

"My opinion," he wrote, "is that the bird in the Luneau video is a normal Pileated Woodpecker."

Beyond the footage itself, Jackson was more broadly concerned by the fluctuating details of Gallagher and Harrison's initial sighting, particularly the ever-decreasing distance between Gallagher and what he'd seen in the swamp that day. What was once estimated to be eighty feet away was later shortened to seventy feet, then shortened again to sixty-five feet. Jackson conceded that these observational variances hardly disproved the sighting, but they did spur an important question: "How many of us could accurately judge the distance to a bird flying across an open space, having seen it for mere seconds and from a moving canoe?"

Borrowing from Nixonian semantics, Jackson concluded that "mistakes were made" but blamed not only scientists, but also the "government, media, and the public relying on the combined authority of the Cornell Laboratory and *Science*."

The root of the problem ran much deeper than a blurry video or fluctuating details; it was that everyone—myself included—was quick to believe what nobody could quite prove: that the bird was unequivocally back. Optimism, overzealousness, and a moving target with a twin had created the conditions for a proverbial case of "putting the cart before the horse," or, in this case, the bird before the burden of proof.

Yet before condemning the search, consider the alternative: a scenario in which, despite a smattering of alleged sightings, the scientific community chose to do nothing. What if they had simply ignored the sightings for fear of risking their reputations? Though the Recovery Team's findings would indeed disappoint, wouldn't we be more disappointed by a scientific community unwilling to take the risk?

After all, there was so much to potentially gain.

First and foremost, a rediscovery of Ivory-billed Woodpecker proportions would've likely served as a much-needed game change for state and federally funded environmental agencies, whose budgets often find their way to the chopping block. Not only that, but the Endangered Species Act—"a law that is perhaps nearly as endangered as this super-rare woodpecker," wrote scientist David Blockstein in 2005—would potentially have gained renewed support.

Moreover, the Ivory-bills' reemergence wouldn't have just benefited their species but would likely have laid the groundwork to benefit an array of species by refocusing America's attention on the importance of wildlife preserves. Even without a confirmed bird, a 2015 article in *BirdWatching* reported that from 2003 to 2013, thirteen million dollars of state and federal funds were allocated for land acquisition to protect the Ivory-bills' habitat—a significant portion of the twenty million spent throughout the decade on the bird. Even if there were no Ivory-bills left to protect, an acquisition of such magnitude certainly helped protect other species within that habitat, though critics argue this money might've been better spent to more directly assist other species in need.

When moving beyond the interconnectedness between the ecological and the economic, I'm still faced with a more fundamental question: Didn't most bird-loving scientists *want* to believe in the bird's return? And if so, did their desire cloud their judgment?

"We all want there to be Ivory-billed woodpeckers out there," Jackson confirmed in his 2006 article. "We all have hope."

What the Recovery Team didn't have, however, was irrefutable proof.

Meanwhile, Harley didn't even have hope.

Though I know of only two ways an African Grey parrot can end its life—(1) by offering itself to a predator and (2) by self-mutilating— Harley took it upon himself to try both.

He'd seemed to attempt the first option the previous spring, when, following an afternoon spent bobbing along a branch in a backyard tree, our bird was targeted and dive-bombed by a hawk. Despite the brief struggle that ensued, the hawk's talons missed their mark, and Harley—having witnessed his life flashing before his beady little eyes— hobbled his way shamefully back to the house.

He selected a day or so before Christmas to attempt the second option, and this time, his trouble appeared to pay off.

Well, almost.

Sometime before carving the Christmas ham my mother walked into the living room to find Harley burbling blood from his wings, the molt of his plume drifting like snow dust against the backdrop of glowing bulbs.

My dad was nowhere to be found (last-minute shopping, perhaps, or entranced in a motorcycle showroom), and so it fell upon me to accompany my mother and Harley to the emergency animal hospital. I sat in the backseat with my hand pressed to the top of the cardboard box, listening to Harley's claws scratch from within. A peek inside revealed a parrot drunk on blood loss, bobbing his head and pecking at his chest. Every time the car turned, his body skittered across the bottom of the box with the grace of an air hockey puck. His brain may have been the size of a walnut, but he was smart enough not to fight inertia.

Through the square of light at the top of the box, I glanced down at that pitiful creature trapped in his blood-soaked prison.

You did this to yourself, I thought.

But as we pulled into the gray-slushed parking lot of the animal hospital, I realized he'd done it to *us* as well.

That bird brought no tidings of good cheer, but another message: *Merry Christmas, assholes.*

Thankfully, for a generation of searchers, the Ivory-billed Woodpecker has sent a more optimistic message: *Find me, I'm out here somewhere; you need only keep looking.*

Many of today's most committed Ivory-bill searchers trace their first encounter with the bird to Don Moser's 1972 *LIFE* magazine article "The Last Ivory Bill"—an immersive, journalistic adventure into the swamplands of Texas and South Carolina. Throughout the article, Moser and his trusted guide, naturalist John Dennis, dedicate weeks to their pursuit, though ultimately spot no thought-to-be extinct birds.

Upon first reading Moser's work, I find myself most interested by how little the motives of Ivory-bill searchers seem to have evolved over the past forty years. Much like today, those who searched did so for different reasons: money, fame, as well as grasping a handhold on what Moser describes as one of the most "powerful political levers in saving a threatened wilderness."

"And there is something else," Moser writes. "Partly because the bird is so beautiful and we destroyed it, it comes back to haunt us."

Translation: we are searching for redemption as much as a bird.

Moser calls the Ivory-bill a "symbol"—living proof, perhaps, "of all those creatures we have sent down the road to extinction." But the bird's reemergence, he poeticizes, might also symbolize "that country inside us where a panther stretches in the sun."

His description gives me pause, forcing me to reconsider where the rare and the regal currently take refuge in our world.

My mind drifts first to Francis Zirrer—more rare than regal—whose deep love for nature allowed him his own backwoods refuge in the wilds of Wisconsin. Next it drifts to Moser's guide, John Dennis, a man whom Moser describes as "dogged," one who "plodded the woods . . . like a farmer on his back 40." Like Zirrer, Dennis was seemingly at ease with himself in the woods, though when he left the woods, he—like any other endangered species—was left exposed.

After making public an alleged Ivory-bill sighting in 1966, followed two years later by an alleged sound recording, Dennis's own credibility was called into question. The knockout blow came from Ivory-bill scholar James Tanner himself, who gave little credence to Dennis's claims.

"Dennis badly wants to find ivorybills," Tanner said, "when he says he has seen them, he believes he has seen them—but he hasn't."

Moser attempts to defend his guide's honor, though by article's end tries a new tack:

"Perhaps it didn't matter whether Dennis found the bird or not. What did matter was that he continued looking."

This is the moment Moser's article reaches its crescendo, the culminating paragraph that reads like a battle cry, not only to defend a bird, but to defend the wilds of our unchartered imagination.

"In a way," Moser remarks, "the bird means more as an idea than it ever could as a reality. A real ivory bill would be observed and trailed, reported upon in scientific journals and the popular press."

Moser makes clear that he hopes the bird might be spared such a fate, one in which the unfortunate creature would undoubtedly be appraised, saddled with a price tag, and then reduced to a political football or science experiment. Simply put, he didn't want the Lord God Bird reduced "from a myth and a metaphor to a curiosity."

"If the question of its existence remains unanswered," he concludes, "it will continue to range the back country of the mind, and those who wish to trail it there can find it in their visions."

Yet Moser's powerful language does little to counteract his heart-breaking message:

That quite likely, the only refuge for these birds remains only in our heads.

While human action dramatically contributed to the demise of the Ivory-billed Woodpecker, we can hardly be blamed for Harley's rash behavior—at least not humans on the whole.

My family, however, can certainly shoulder a bit of blame for our bird's unhappiness. As penance, following Harley's self-inflicted feather extractions, Mom and I held vigil in the emergency animal hospital throughout that cold December evening. After half an hour or so, we were joined by a few hand-wringing cat owners so lost in their own drama that they could hardly pay attention to ours. We didn't mind the anonymity; we welcomed it.

"Haven't spent Christmas in the animal E.R. for a while now," I joked to my mother, which in truth wasn't a joke at all. A decade prior Santa had seen fit to place a box turtle beneath the tree, though he'd failed to test its temperament prior to doing so. If he had, perhaps he'd have learned that our box turtle fancied himself a snapping turtle and aimed to prove it; mainly by attaching himself to my mother's finger for most of the morning.

It was a memorable Christmas, one that forced us to ask ourselves the hard questions, such as: *Is this the kind of thing you go to the human hospital for, or the animal hospital?*

Ten years later, as Mom and I slouched in the animal hospital chairs yet again, there was no need for that question. We were there because Harley hated us; so much, in fact, that he preferred death to imagining his life with us.

Though my father loved Harley unconditionally (his bandaged fingers served as proof), the rest of us did not. In our opinion, that bird went out of his way to try our patience, a blitzkrieg of feathers whose carefully planned airstrikes often resulted in shit stains on my mother's carpets and punctures in my brother's clothes. He was relentless, and even after our halfhearted attempts to clip his feathers, he'd still continue his aerial assaults, regularly crashing beak first into the curtains or getting tangled in the blinds.

Despite it all, as my mother and I held vigil for him, I tried to forgive Harley his trespasses. Prayed he might forgive ours as well. And half an hour later, when the vet called us into the sterile room, I was glad to find Harley still alive.

"He'll be fine," the vet assured us, but then rephrased: "Well, maybe not *fine*, but he's not going to die tonight."

The vet told us things we mostly already knew—how easy it was for African Greys to become depressed, and how it was our job as his family to do what we could to make him feel at home.

But it's not his home, I thought, staring out at our snow-capped car in the lot. *This isn't even his continent.*

It's not easy being alone, which is where more and more Ivory-bill believers began finding themselves as Rohrbaugh's search team struggled to find definitive proof.

Fourteen years after Moser's article hit newsstands, naturalist Michael Harwood provided his own updated account of the conservation status of the species.

His 1986 *Audubon* article—provocatively titled "You Can't Protect What Isn't There"—sought to dismiss the many so-called myths associated with the bird, including the "myth" that Pileated Woodpeckers and their Ivory-bill cousins are all but indistinguishable.

"That's baloney," he wrote, adding that misidentifications often occur as a result of one of three shortcomings: a lack of birding experience by the spotter, a lack of care, or an abundance of wishful thinking.

Surely the members of the search team knew their birds and took care in their pursuit. Which leads us to Harwood's third criteria for misidentification: did they simply wish too hard?

While the more conspiratorial fringes of the scientific blogosphere have argued that the bird's "rediscovery" was nothing more than a publicity stunt (or worse, a false catalyst to entice donors), the more credible voices of the ornithological world side with a gentler explanation.

"It has nothing to do with honesty or expertise or truthfulness," David Sibley was quoted saying in a 2006 *National Geographic* article. "We all make these kinds of mistakes. We get excited about a possibility, and our brain tends to jump to that possibility whenever we see something remotely similar."

A few months prior, Sibley had offered a bit more detail on how a mistake of this magnitude might have been made. *New York Times* writer Jack Hitt paraphrases Sibley's theory: how as the inventory project's inner circle grew, those in the know fell victim to "a kind of groupthink, leading to wishful sightings."

It would hardly have been the first time a bevy of birders had been bamboozled.

In his introduction to *Sibley's Birding Basics*, Sibley concedes that bird identification is "rarely 100 percent certain."

Thus, he explains, when a mistake is made, the birder must learn from it.

"Perhaps you were just being lazy," he writes, "perhaps jumping to conclusions on limited data, or perhaps you were misled because the bird was unusual."

And finally, a prophetic chiding that seems to speak directly to the Ivory-bill controversy:

"Talking yourself into something or denying your mistakes will only slow the learning process and cause problems in the long run."

Equally prophetic was Michael Harwood's article, in which he wrote—nearly two decades prior to David Luneau's 2004 footage—that "you couldn't satisfy the doubters, I believe, even with a videotape of a bird in motion."

This certainly proved true—Luneau's video clip now serves as Exhibit A for believers and doubters alike.

What one sees, it seems, depends in part on what one *wants* to see.

Though I know what I want to see, I've now replayed the video far too many times to offer anything of value. Instead, I return my attention to the Harwood article, and there, buried in his doom and gloom, I spot a silver lining.

"Serious hunting for ivorybills in this country will be left mainly to the young, the non-professional, and the enthusiastic."

I smile.

At last I'm being recognized for my strengths.

That last Christmas with Harley, we tried to take the vet's advice by including him in our family activities. Though admittedly, his self-harm had served to dramatically weaken our yuletide cheer. In an effort to finish us off, upon his return from the vet he immediately pooped on our Santa puzzle, then tore the roof off of our gingerbread house.

Of course, he also continued his regularly scheduled disruptions: a rush of dive-bombings, most of which concluded with his getting tangled in the blinds. When he tired of our untangling him, he committed himself to strutting around the house like an angry dinosaur on the verge of extinction, rotating between squawking at the dog and the piano bench, both of which refused to move out of his way.

What Harley learned to love most in the world was the mirror behind the kitchen table. He'd often brave the entire expanse of the living room—past the perils of our other pets—for a chance to say hello to his new best friend. They had so much in common, and we convinced ourselves it wasn't cruelty if it managed to ease his pain. Some days during winter break I'd watch him press his beak to his reflection, then listen guiltily as he trilled his haunting songs to himself for hours. He interspersed a few clucks between the warbles, which I translated as an S.O.S. to his doppelgänger to get him the hell out of here fast.

Eventually we heard him, and my father agreed to hand him off to a woman who specialized in exotic birds. She promised she'd give Harley a good home, which was more than we could give him.

We let him go and called it mercy, though more likely, we just wanted off the hook. We didn't want to be responsible for causing that bird any more heartache. We had enough bird blood on our hands as it was.

Harley—though no Ivory-billed Woodpecker—spent most every moment of his life with us unaware that there were others like him. Aside from the occasional YouTube clip, the only company he enjoyed was with the African Grey in the mirror.

"Hello, pretty bird," he'd call to himself again and again. "Hello, hello."

Years later, when I'd think back on those moments, that bird, I'd think also of the alleged Ivory-billed Woodpecker caught on David Luneau's tape.

And I'd wonder which of the two birds had it worse: the one who was lonely, or the one who, at best, was alone.

5

The Life List

For thirty-plus years I have probed the forests, fields, and shores in an effort to be nearer birds, and each year I find them more and more elusive.
—Steve Betchkal, "Personal Extinction," in *Make Birds Not War*, 2011

In the mid-1800s, when Italian engineer Ignazio Porro first conceived of his right-angled prism designs, he could hardly imagine the impact his optics would have on the world. In fact, during his lifetime, Porro's relative obscurity only further solidified his status as a mostly unknown inventor, one who died impoverished in 1875. Yet today the Porro prism remains one of two predominant prism systems routinely utilized in modern binoculars, refracting the light and flipping the image until it brings the distant world close.

Though invented just a few decades later, the alternative roof prism design has only become popularized for birders in recent years. Rather than relying upon two separate prisms to bounce light, the roof prism streamlines the process. The result is a more compact model of binocular, one that, according to most birders, produces a higher-quality image.

Steve Betchkal wants to be sure I can see the difference for myself, so he invites me to his home one cool Saturday morning in November.

A knock, and a few moments later, Steve whirs around the corner, a look of surprise on his face.

"Did you ring the bell?" he asks, swinging the door wide.

"Nah, just knocked."

"Huh. I didn't even hear you," he says. "Good thing I saw you, huh?"

I nod, withholding a smile as I realize he's identified me the way he might a bird: relying upon sight since I offered no song to assist.

As he welcomes me in, my eyes catch the American Eagle logo affixed to his gray sweater, the first of many inanimate birds I'm destined to spot throughout his household.

"This way," he says. "I got the tour set up right in here."

He leads me to his dining room table, upon which sit four pairs of binoculars alongside a black duffel.

"This is what I currently use," he says, directing me to the first pair. "They're called the Vortex Vipers."

I nod as if this means something to me.

"They're roof prisms," he says, introducing me to the term, "while these," he continues, picking up an older pair, "are Porro prisms."

The Porros are bulky in my hands, the kind of optics I'd expect to find in an exhibit on birding rather than on a modern expedition. Of course, saying so publicly would border on sacrilege to the Porro faithful, many of whom swear by the brighter image.

"These old-fashioned Porros," Steve explains, "they have some . . . disadvantages."

"Were these your first pair?" I ask.

"No, they're just a symbolic pair. But my original pair looked just like 'em. They were 7x35s, too. Nearly identical."

"7x35?"

The first number refers to magnification power, he explains, while the second refers to the diameter of the objective lens.

"When you're deciding on a pair," he tells me, "be sure to divide the second number by the first. You'll want it to be around five or so."

As a prospective buyer, I file away this information for later.

"So how much do a pair generally go for?" I ask, a little afraid of the answer.

"Well, the ones I've got now, the Vipers, they cost me around seven hundred," he says.

My wallet winces.

"But even roof prisms in the three-hundred range are very good," he's quick to add. "You can go all the way up to twenty-five hundred dollars a pair, but every time I get tempted, I think, *Man, for that kind of money you could take an exotic vacation and see all kinds of exotic birds . . .*"

Which is how Steve prefers to spend his money.

In the winter of 2012 he and his wife, Julie, splurged on a birding trip to Costa Rica.

Correction: Steve splurged on a birding trip to Costa Rica, while Julie—who claims she is no birder, though Steve believes otherwise— agreed to come along. The trip proved life changing for Steve, motivating him to continue planning international bird-related travel whenever time and money allowed. In fact, as we examine his table full of binoculars, Steve informs me that he and his wife are planning to visit Mexico within a few months' time.

"I may not add any birds to my life list while I'm down there," he admits, lowering expectations, "but I guess we'll have to wait and see."

For the uninitiated, the birder's "life list" is exactly what it sounds like: a list of birds spotted over a lifetime. While some lists consist of little more than a tick on a checklist, for folks like Steve, who value the memory of each encounter, the lists can be meticulous and complex undertakings, written snapshots to record the experience in full.

Though no experience can be recorded in full without the proper binoculars, which is why I dedicate half an hour or so getting to know the various types, familiarizing myself with their weight and functionality as Steve and I aim our respective pairs toward the neighbor's house.

"So clear," I say as I make my way to the Vipers. "It's like looking at the world in HD."

"That's it exactly," he agrees, returning another pair to the table. "And if you like those, make sure to look through one of the twenty-five-hundred-dollar pairs if you ever get a chance. It feels like you're going to have an orgasm," he laughs.

Next he takes me through his duffel, or as he calls it, his "grab and go" pack.

"Sometimes I'll be online and I'll see a message about some rare bird nearby, so I just grab this bag and head out the door," he explains. "It happens all the time."

Whereas birding once demanded equal parts shoe leather and luck, the tech-savvy twenty-first-century birder can now rely upon bird-tracking websites, thereby diminishing the need for both. Though the birding community's collective reconnaissance has been a boon for birders, these real-time reports often prove too tantalizing for folks like Steve.

"It's especially a problem when you see reports from Milwaukee," Steve says. "You see it and think, *Oh, maybe I should make a quick four-hour drive to check it out . . .*"

On occasion he's made similarly distant drives, knowing full well there's no guarantee that the bird in question will be waiting for him upon his arrival.

"Does that happen?" I ask. "People drive all this way only to come up empty-handed?"

"Oh sure," he shrugs. "Happens a lot."

I smile at the Zen-like quality of his acceptance.

"You know," I say, treading lightly, "it seems like there's a fine line between being an enthusiastic birder and . . . well, an obsessive one. Where do you fit on the spectrum?"

"Oh, I'm just obsessed," he confirms. "But obsession can be good. I like to say that obsession is good in moderation. I mean we all seek abundance in everything. When taken to excess we call that greed, but really the living human spirit wants abundances. We want an abundance of feeling, an abundance of family, an abundance of the good things in life. And that's what the best of birding's all about," he tells me point-blank. "It's about the abundance of good things, of seeing things that make you feel joyous."

It's hard to put into words the joy that birds bring to one's life. Surely it differs for everyone. While some enjoy the beauty of the birds themselves, others enjoy the journey to find them, a journey that generally serves as a convenient entry point into nature, an excuse to tromp the wilds for a while, or at least peer into our own backyards.

I first began my own backyard peering one recent spring after hearing what sounded like a flame of eagles circling my pines. Day after day, I stared into the trees to find nothing; that is, until my backyard neighbor clued me in to the source of the sound.

"The crows are merciless," my neighbor explained, "plucking baby birds right out of the nest. Which is why we set up the speakers," he said, nodding to a black box balanced on his windowsill. "So if you think you're hearing eagles, you probably are."

I most certainly was, their cries replaying every time the crows came home to roost. For a few days my neighbor's eagle recording seemed to scare them straight, though after a while, they grew wise to the ruse.

I'm more than a little embarrassed to admit that it took a phalanx of fake birds to fully introduce me to the real ones. Embarrassed, too, to concede that had it not been for my neighbor's anticrow sound system, I might've continued to overlook the daily dramas playing out in my own backyard.

I suppose I take some comfort in knowing that I'm hardly alone in my trespass. As Ralph Waldo Emerson wrote, "few adult persons can see nature," adding also that the true "lover of nature" is one who has "retained the spirit of infancy even into the era of manhood."

But how is one to have it both ways—to maintain the pragmatism of adulthood and the wonder of a child?

The birds have helped a great deal, serving as my near constant reminder of the natural splendor that surrounds me, while also doing much to sharpen my observational skills.

By midsummer, I'd grown accustomed to noticing far more than just crows. I'd begun noticing the robins, too, as well as a variety of woodpeckers (disappointedly, not an Ivory-bill among them). One day, on a whim, I refilled the birdfeeder left behind by our home's previous owners. Then, for many days following, I watched the nightly return of the Black-capped Chickadees while rinsing dishes in the sink.

Summer swept into fall, and still I watched, hypnotized by the dark swirl of crows that continued to mass in the trees. They watched me too, licking their beaks, so to speak, as my fifteen-pound Chihuahua and I took our morning constitutional around the block. Suddenly we, too, were part of the drama, their confidence growing along with their numbers. By mid-October, it was hardly unusual for my dog and me to endure the taunts issuing forth from their roost in the murder tree.

That's what we came to call it: the murder tree. Not only because a group of crows is technically that—a murder—but also because they appeared to have a hit out on my dog. The leaves were all but gone by then, leaving behind skeletal branches weighed down by that cloud of head-bobbing birds.

Caw, caw! they'd cry.

"Go climb a tree!" I'd shout (though of course, they were one step ahead of me).

By midwinter their shade drew a stark contrast with the snow, though they still somehow made themselves invisible. Some days I'd walk beneath a branch full of those birds and wouldn't even notice until after I'd passed.

One morning, pre-coffee, I spotted the slightest movement in the pines behind my house.

I rubbed my eyes and saw a crow.

Rubbed them again and saw two crows.

Rubbed them once more and saw fifty.

They exploded like Roman candles, feathered balls firing forth in a dozen different directions, setting the tree to trembling.

It was ghastly, gorgeous, sublime.

Despite their occasional flourishes of beauty, those crows brought me no joy.

What they brought me was closer to nature.

By threatening my dog they'd forced me to remain on high alert, prompting me to leave the earbuds at home and pay attention to the birds in those branches. I'd been living among them my entire life, yet unless one saw fit to shit on my shoulder or dive-bomb my dog, I'd rarely paid them any heed.

No, the crows brought me no joy, but my noticing did.

And what I noticed was all I'd missed noticing.

I return Steve's binoculars to the table before following him to the pair of twin bookshelves on the opposite side of the room.

"On the left here we have our fiction and nonfiction," Steve explains. "And on the right," he smiles, "we've got our bird books. Some nature, some travel, a few about rock stars on the bottom there, but mostly it's pretty much birds."

Steve snags a Sibley's from the shelf and fans through its worn pages.

"When I was a kid, I'd go through the Penny's and Sears catalogs looking for Christmas gifts," he says. "And it's sort of the same with these guides. Some nights I'll pull one off the shelf and just look at the birds' colors. To me, this is like Christmas. I'll look at a bird and think, *I want that for Christmas! I want to see that bird!*"

He directs me to his "Christmas wish list" within the book's pages: the Superb Fruit Dove, the Crimson Rosella, among others. As he pages through, I see most of these birds for the first time, their spectacular designs all but otherworldly.

"So colorful," Steve says, hypnotized. "They're like . . . candy with wings."

He returns the Sibley's to the shelf and reaches for a travel guide.

"In preparation for a birding trip," he continues, "I always study hard. For me, it's like taking a class."

He points to his heavily annotated pages, the marks of a dutiful student.

"The trick is to know what to look for *before* you get there," he explains. "And not just birds, but habitats, too. The whole idea is to find the habitat. When you find the right habitat, that's when you find the right bird."

Bird-watching, Steve explains, is in many ways a study in ecosystems.

And in order to understand the fauna, it's best to know a bit about the flora, too.

"And when you get a sense of it all," he continues, "when you watch birds bonding with their environment, everything just becomes . . . perfect. Suddenly it all just meshes."

"You make birding sound like a gateway drug," I joke. "You begin with the birds, but pretty soon you find yourself interested in their habitats. Next thing you know you're into the plants, the flowers, the trees . . ."

"Oh, absolutely," Steve says. "And you've got to understand all of it. In Costa Rica, for instance, the quetzals like these little avocados. So you don't go roaming the hills in search of quetzals, you go straight to the avocado groves."

"So when we destroy a bird's habitat," I say, extending the logic, "do the birds generally go with it?"

"That can definitely happen," Steve agrees. "Habitat's everything."

I think of the Singer Tract, the donkey engine, Eckelberry's Ivory-bill preening herself in the tree.

I expect our conversation to turn toward my beloved spark bird, but Steve references another bird instead: "Have you heard of the Dusky Seaside Sparrow?"

Of course I haven't, though I take a moment to pretend to mull it over.

"Well, basically they got wiped out by a single hurricane," Steve explains.

Further research mostly confirms the story. The part that Steve forgets, however, is that the "hurricane" was actually the human-induced flooding of Merritt Island—the only place on earth the nonmigratory birds called home. The flooding was an attempt to reduce mosquito populations during the construction of the Kennedy Space Center, though as NASA attempted to kill one species, they inadvertently killed an unrelated subspecies, instead.

Of course, no extinction story is ever so simple, and as noted previously, to understand a species' extinction fully, we must consider both ultimate and proximate causes. According to *Palm Beach Sun Sentinel* writer Tom Sander, about 70 percent of Duskies were initially killed during the "'mosquito eradication program' of the 1940s." Following the population's dramatic decline, those that remained died during the island's subsequent flooding, then the river's dredging, and finally as a result of land developers' commitment to transforming a marsh into a subdivision.

Ultimately, we killed them, and proximately, we pretty much killed them, too.

While Sander acknowledges humankind's role in the bird's demise, he also attempts a cost-benefit analysis.

"Is the world better or worse off today because the Kennedy Space Center was built, because its workers had highways to drive on and homes to live in?" Sander asks. "The answer is obvious."

Maybe for him; but for me—the newest groupie in the Dusky Seaside Sparrow fan club—it's hard to trivialize their extinction, particularly given that it was caused, at least in part, by our own poor planning.

As if to lessen the tragedy, Sander reminds readers that we sent the last one off in style.

"At the end," Sander writes, "the last dusky was treated like royalty, kept in a special 8-by-10-foot cage, cooled and bathed by a soft artificial rainfall, fed a particularly nutritious diet of crickets, seeds and grubs and protected from infection by a requirement that his human guardians disinfect their boots every time they came to pay a visit."

Yet these extravagant gestures seem farcical given the utter disregard with which we'd treated the subspecies previously.

In 1983 the four remaining specimens were transported to Disney's Discovery Island nature reserve, where they indeed lived out their days in ease. There was nothing to be done; the last female had died four years prior, and extinction was a foregone conclusion.

One by one the remaining males drifted into death, until at last Orange Band—the recipient of the aforementioned royal treatment—died on June 17, 1987.

Since news of the Duskies had yet to make it to *Sesame Street*, I—a toddler at the time—remained wholly unaware of their destruction. (In those days, I admit, most of my concern for birds began and ended with Big Bird himself.) However, upon reflecting on the Duskies' story today, it's disconcerting for me to realize that I once shared the planet with a creature no longer here.

Equally disconcerting are the color photographs of the bird that remain. A part of me wants desperately to believe that extinction is somehow anachronistic in the modern era, just some antiquated practice from our past. But even if we could somehow persuade ourselves of that fairy tale, the color photos serve as incontrovertible proof.

You've heard a version of this story before:

Once upon a time there lived a bird, and before he stopped living, we snapped his picture.

Of course, you don't need a camera to remember a bird; all you need is a life list.

Or, in Steve's case, several life lists.

"You have to understand," Steve says as I follow him into his basement, "that my lists are very unique to me. Not only do I have my own three-letter coding system, but I also have point values for birds based on how hard they are to find."

Okay, I think. *Well, that doesn't sound so complicated.*

"It's an eight-point scale," he clarifies.

Oh.

In the days leading up to my visit with Steve, I humbled myself by reading Bill Thompson's *Bird Watching for Dummies.*

Though I resent the title's implication, I admit it's got me pegged.

According to Thompson, when it comes to life lists, "no rules exist," though he still manages to fill an entire chapter with "suggestions" on how one might consider maintaining one.

Though I repeat: no rules *technically* exist.

Which is good news for Steve, whose complex system of lists couldn't be cracked with an Enigma machine. In addition to the intricacy of his three-letter coding and eight-point scale, his data is further encrypted by a unique dating system.

"I started birding in 1979," he says as he opens an Excel sheet, "so that was Year 1."

Which makes 2014 Year 36.

In the time between—according to his life list—Steve has success-fully spotted 636 different species of North American birds and 936 worldwide. Both are impressive numbers, though Steve brushes off any praise.

"What's more interesting," he says as he scrolls down the screen, "is that when you start to analyze the numbers, there are more and more gaps over the years. It's getting harder and harder to find birds. Just look at this Bay-breasted Warbler," he says, pointing to a cell on the spreadsheet. "That's two years of misses right here. And see that gap for the Cerulean Warbler? And this Cape May . . . look at this," he says, "two misses in the last six years!"

For me—staring blankly at a mostly indecipherable spreadsheet—this hardly seems cause for alarm. But it's clear that Steve feels otherwise. As someone who's literally watching birds vanish before his eyes, he knows the gaps in his sightings speak volumes.

"So is this your problem or the world's problem?" I ask.

"This is the world's problem," he says, turning from the screen to face me. "I'm out there looking."

Most troubling for Steve is the recent decline in Purple Martin sightings here in Wisconsin.

"In 2013—for the first time in my life—I didn't see one. I couldn't find a single one in the entire state. This is a bird I was raised with," he says, "a bird I love, and I couldn't find one anywhere."

Steve walks me through his various lists—life list, state list, county list, backyard list, even his wife's list (which, since she's not a birder, he maintains on her behalf). Each is not only a testament to his role as a citizen scientist, but a testament to his role as a storyteller, too. By clicking on the species name, one can read the details of up to fifty individual sightings per bird. And not just the day and time, but the location as well, often down to the cross streets.

"Why fifty?" I ask. "Why list fifty separate sightings of a single species before hanging it up?"

"If you see a bird fifty times, it's kind of like you've gotten to know them personally," he explains. "By then you'll know them by their song, their flight pattern, you know them in all kinds of ways. If you're just a lister, you'd say, 'All right, I've seen one. I'm done.' But to me, I look at that and I think, *Well, that's just a one-night stand.*

"There's no intimacy there," I say.

"None! And the intimacy is what's so important to me. I'd love to see enough Baird's Sparrows so that I can look at one and say, 'I know your song, your call note when you're in the grass. I know it's you. I know *you*.'"

I dreamy smile crosses his face.

"So are your lists for you or for conservation purposes?

"Both. But you know, the funny thing about all this," he says, reality setting in, "is that when I die, this stuff will all be erased. There will be no point to it. Unless one of my kids says, 'This will be fun to keep for family history—all my dad's eccentric notes about birds!' they won't be kept at all. I've done all this work over the years, and it probably doesn't matter to anybody but me."

"The coding system does seem a bit . . . complex," I admit. "Is it because the information is personal to you?"

"No," he says, "it's because it doesn't matter. No one else is going to read it. I can make it as complicated as I want."

And then, a silence so deep I dare not say a word.

"But . . . it's still fun," he softens, offering me a half smile. "I wouldn't do it if it wasn't fun."

How you see a bird depends on how you view it: whether it's with binoculars, the naked eye, or by staring at a screen.

In the months leading up to his Costa Rica trip, Steve settled for the third option, studying an assortment of birds through the glow of his basement computer screen. He'd click one picture after another, meticulously taking notes on each bird's unique features, its habitats, its songs. It's easy to envision him peering hard at the screen, adjusting his glasses and jotting details in his notebooks. But it's equally easy to envision him on his upstairs couch, pulling one book after another from his bird bookshelf and basking in their many colorful images.

When I ask him how much of birding comes down to looking and how much comes down to luck, he says it's a little of both.

"People tend to enjoy birding at different levels," he says. "Sometimes people just play it by chance encounter, and that's fun. But I think it's also important to be educated about what you're looking for. Because when that bird pops up I want to say, 'I've heard about you! I know you from what I've seen, what I've read, and now I get to meet you.'"

He reminds me of the brevity of our interactions with birds; how in some cases, we get no more than five seconds with a species in our lifetime.

"And if that's all the time you get, then you don't want to waste a single second flipping through your guidebook trying to figure out what it is. You want to be able to say, 'I just saw a Red-capped Manakin, or a Rufous-throated Solitaire.' That's why you study in advance."

To do otherwise, Steve says, is a disservice to the bird.

"If you waste those five seconds, then you've failed that bird. Because that bird was introducing itself, and you blew it, pal."

Shamefaced, I think of all the brief interactions with birds that I've surely blown. All those earbudded dog walks that inadvertently insulated me from the natural world.

Steve clicks through a few more files before coming to his Costa Rica audio clips.

"Check this out," he whispers, fiddling with the volume. "Ferruginous Pygmy-Owl."

There, in his dimly lit basement, we tilt our ears toward the speaker.

At first, all I hear are the village dogs and the cicadas. But then . . .

Hoohoohoohoohoohoohooo . . .

The high-pitched sound of what might otherwise be a squeaky wheel.

Hoohoohoohoohoohoohooo . . .

"This was just before dawn," Steve whispers. "He was calling just outside my room."

Next he clicks on a clip to play the deep-throated holler of a howler monkey, a sound I never dreamed I'd hear in a basement in Eau Claire.

"When you're in the dark and the howler monkey goes off," Steve says, "it's just one of those singular experiences, you know?"

I nod. I get it.

"There's just one more I want to share with you," he says, clicking deeper into various folders. "Here."

I expect another howler monkey, or a Pygmy Owl, or some other resident of the Costa Rican wilderness.

Instead, he gives me the ocean, the soothing exhalation of surf rushing across stones.

"It sounds just the way it did a thousand years ago," Steve marvels. "No development, no people, no nothing. Imagine yourself there."

As I do, I can't help but also imagine the seabirds hovering overhead, floating like kites before landing on the rock cliff just behind me.

I listen closely to the final rush of the final wave before the audio clip cuts out.

Steve minimizes the clip, but before he does, I see it's dated: February 1, 2012.

"You've preserved that moment forever," I tell him, "Or at least 'till your hard drive dies."

"Yeah," he laughs, satisfied. "I guess I have."

But he's preserved far more than just that. By way of his audio clips, his photos, and his life lists, he's preserved his encounters with tens of thousands of birds, all of which, when taken together, offers me his unintentional autobiography. Like a good pair of binoculars, Steve has brought the wild world close, introducing me to an assortment of birds, many of which I'll never know in nature.

With the rush of the waves still ringing in my ears, we start back up the stairs. As we do, Steve reminds me that birding's not all fun and games. Though he's had quite a bit of success at it, he's also paid a price.

"Honestly, I'm lonely a lot of the time," he admits. "There are times when I'm birding where I become very possessive of my moments. I don't *want* anyone to intrude. But," he continues, "there are other times when you see a bird and all you want to do is toast a beer with somebody and talk about it."

I tell him I'm good for that much, and that we can toast birds together at the conclusion of our previously planned bird survey—better known as a Christmas Count—set for early January.

"Sounds good," Steve smiles as he walks me toward the door. "I'll look forward to it."

As I start outside, a crow cawing from a nearby tree immediately accosts me.

Instinctively, I quicken my pace.

What I wouldn't give, I think as I walk toward my car, *if you were a Dusky Seaside Sparrow, instead.*

6

The Professor and the Pigeon

For one species to mourn the death of another is a new thing under the sun. The Cro-Magnon who slew the last mammoth thought only of steaks. The sportsman who shot the last pigeon thought only of his prowess. The sailor who clubbed the last auk thought of nothing at all. But we, who have lost our pigeons, mourn the loss. Had the funeral been ours, the pigeons would hardly have mourned us.
—Aldo Leopold, "On A Monument to the Pigeon," 1947

I'm woken at dawn by a tapping on my face.

Woodpecker, I think sleepily.

I've been dreaming them for weeks, entire flocks of Downies and Hairies and Pileateds and Ivory-bills, all of them dive-bombing my subconscious.

I swat at the tapper in question, though, undeterred, it continues—prompting me to crack one eye, then the other, and face the source of the tapping. It's not a woodpecker but my two-and-a-half-year-old son, Henry, thwacking me with the remote.

"Daddy," he says—*tap, tap*—"let's watch *Sesame Street*."

It's not how I'd planned to spend Saturday morning, but since I know of no other way to get the tapping to stop, I tuck him in alongside me.

"Okay," I sigh, prying the remote from his hand and scanning through our options. "Which episode do you want?"

I don't let him answer. Instead, I spot the word "pigeon" in a synopsis and choose that episode for us both.

Suddenly I'm wide awake, sitting upright with a notebook and scrawling as fast as Bert can bestow his bird-related knowledge. He's decked out in birding gear—from the top of his safari hat down to the binoculars dangling round his neck. Apparently Bert is in search of a Blue Bar Pigeon, the last of the seven Rock Pigeons on his life list.

Great, I think, *even a Muppet's got a longer life list than me . . .*

From our place on the bed, Henry and I watch as Bert explains his trouble to Elmo and Abby, at last moaning, "Oh, I'll never find that Blue Bar Pigeon!"

"Why don't you make it interesting," I shout at the screen, "try searching for an Ivory-bill."

"Yeah!" Henry echoes with equal disdain. "An Ibery-brill!"

As a distraught Bert stomps off stage right, Elmo and Abby decide to assist him in spotting his elusive bird. And so the duo begin their circuitous quest, wandering from one misidentification to another—a plotline clearly borrowed from my own life.

First, the Muppets encounter a chickadee.

"If you're looking for a pigeon," the chickadee remarks, "then you're looking for a bird that's bigger than me."

Next, they meet a robin.

"Were you looking for a bird with a beautiful red breast?" she inquires (and the answer, of course, is no).

Finally, they encounter a brusque, Brooklyn-accented Blue Jay.

"Me? A pigeon?" the Blue Jay scoffs. "Don't be ridi'calous!"

Suffice it to say, by episode's end, Elmo and Abby indeed find their Blue Bar Pigeon, and upon being introduced to his much-sought-after bird, Bert cries, "This is the greatest day of my entire life becaauuuuse . . . I get to do this."

With great gusto, he reaches for his life list of pigeons, adding a final checkmark alongside the picture of the Blue Bar.

Surely this is a momentous occasion in any Muppet's life, and undoubtedly for bird-watching Bert. Yet despite Bert's many pigeon sightings, I know there's one he'll never see.

"What? No Passenger Pigeon?" I heckle Bert.

"Yeah," Henry mocks, "no Passeenjur Pishon!"

I click the remote and watch those Muppets vanish from the screen.

"Come on," I say, lifting Henry from the bed, "time to check the feeders."

Days later, I step onto the University of Wisconsin–Madison campus as the Badger football team pummels the Rutgers Scarlet Knights. It's an away game, thank goodness, which allows my birder brethren and me to find street parking for our slightly less popular Passenger Pigeon Symposium. I step inside Union South, where I soon fade into a crowd of students, all of them dressed in their best Bucky gear, eyes raised toward the TV screens.

I work my way around them—"Excuse me, pardon me, is it this way to the Passenger Pigeon Symposium?"—until at last maneuvering to the second floor's Marquee Theater. A dozen or so folks have already gathered in the foyer, each of them close to doubling me in age.

One by one, the symposium's presenters arrive, beginning with David Blockstein, a former Madisonian now in DC, where he serves as a senior scientist with the National Council for Science and the Environment. I'm familiar with an article he'd written on the Ivory-bill, though since I've never seen him, I draw upon my birding experience and immediately misidentify him.

"Hi there," I say, interrupting Blockstein midbite into his frozen custard cone. "You aren't by chance Stanley Temple?"

I'm referring to *the* Stanley Temple—an emeritus UW professor, Aldo Leopold Foundation Fellow, and resident scholar on all things Passenger Pigeon.

"Nope," Blockstein laughs, taking another bite. "Not me."

He introduces himself, at which point I realize he's one of the day's presenters, and an expert in his own right.

I want to ask him any number of questions about Passenger Pigeons, though since I've already put my foot in my mouth once, I feel it's only fair to allow him to put custard into his. We keep the conversation light, chatting about his homecoming to Wisconsin, which so far has included all the usual rites: brats, Badger football, and Babcock's ice cream.

A few minutes later he points me to the real Stanley Temple. I glance over my shoulder just in time to spot a goateed, middle-aged man drifting past in a suit coat and crisp jeans. He's over six feet tall, imposing, and so focused on final preparations for the symposium that I barely have a chance to shake his hand before he strides away.

"A good guy," Blockstein confirms, taking a final bite of his cone. "And the *real* expert."

No one would dispute him on that.

Stanley Temple has dedicated his life to birds, and by extension, the conservation efforts to protect them. I first heard of him by way of Steve Betchkal, who—as we loitered in the dead bird museum together a few weeks prior—made it clear to me that Stanley Temple was the man to talk to. Or at least listen to, which is all I'd hoped for given he had a symposium to run.

Just shaking his hand is a bit of a thrill, prompting me to wonder if I'd just shaken the hand of a man whose work will be taught in environmental studies classrooms for years to come. Perhaps Temple felt similar awe in holding the professorship that, for thirty-two years, had belonged to Aldo Leopold himself.

For Wisconsin audiences, Aldo Leopold needs no introduction. He remains omnipresent within the state's conservation movement, a man whose eloquent writing on the subject places him on a hallowed bookshelf alongside the likes of John Muir, Wendell Berry, and Rachel Carson, just to name a few. Leopold's impact transcends well beyond Wisconsin, with more than a few folks crediting him for shepherding the environmental movement into the twentieth century. Wisconsin writer Erika Janik calls Leopold "one of the most notable figures of the modern environmental movement," adding that his focus on "preservation, appreciation, and protection of nature" shifted America's philosophy on conservation and likely played a role in the 1973 passage of the Endangered Species Act. His words inspired many, most notably his 1949 nonfiction book *A Sand County Almanac*, which outlines his views on the land ethic, stewardship, and our impact on the natural world.

Including our impact on the Passenger Pigeon.

A few moments after Stanley Temple rushes past, throngs of people begin congregating around the theater's doors. Hundreds gather in the span of a few minutes, a human flock that still pales in comparison to the feathered equivalent that once darkened the skies of the eastern United States.

We take our seats, growing quiet as Temple moves toward the microphone.

"Good afternoon," he says. "Thank you for coming."

From the back, someone shouts the obligatory, "We can't heeeeeeear yooooooooou!"

Temple adjusts, hunching over the lectern to ensure that his words can be heard.

By now, he knows the drill. Over the past year, Temple's taken his show on the road, making good use of the one hundredth anniversary of the passing of the last Passenger Pigeon to share the species' story with the world.

Temple begins by deeming the Passenger Pigeon's demise an "iconic extinction example," adding that their memory provides a "classic teachable moment" for our own "extinction crisis."

Nodding, I scrawl his words as best I can, including his mention of two conservation-minded Wisconsinites who came before: Aldo Leopold and Bill Schorger.

My pen pauses on the second name.

Schorger . . . Schorger . . . I think, my mind scanning its Rolodex.

Suddenly it clicks: Temple's referring to A. W. "Bill" Schorger—the businessman and University of Wisconsin wildlife management professor who, when he wasn't corresponding with hermit Francis Zirrer, was apparently researching Passenger Pigeons.

I had some knowledge of Schorger's interest in the bird, but I hadn't realized that his 1955 book *The Passenger Pigeon: Its Natural History and Extinction* remains the definitive work on the species. As I sit in that auditorium, I can't recall a single reference to Passenger Pigeons anywhere in his letters to Zirrer. Though throughout their correspondence Schorger was certainly mulling the birds' fate, trying to understand how flocks hundreds of miles long could be decimated in such short order; how their conspicuousness likely led to their downfall, their once-vast numbers emboldening men with guns and nets and fire to kill indiscriminately, right up until there were few left to kill.

Nearly sixty years prior to Temple's turn at the lectern, Schorger had already begun framing the tragedy of the Passenger Pigeon as a "classic teachable moment."

"The pigeon was gone but it's passing was a sober lesson to mankind," Schorger wrote. "It brought to sharp attention the fact that a species can become a nonrenewable resource."

It wasn't much, but Schorger's "bird-as-lesson-to-mankind" approach was all the silver lining he could muster. It was a lesson that had cost us a beautiful bird, "the most impressive species of bird that man has ever known," Schorger claimed. "Elegant in form and color, graceful and swift of flight, it moved about and nested in such enormous numbers as to confound the senses." Yet in the very next line, Schorger offset his high praise for the birds by noting their "equally dramatic" disappearance "due to the thoughtless and insatiable greed of man."

You've heard it before, but it bears repeating: in forty years, billions of birds became none.

We took the most abundant bird and made it into a memory.

Stanley Temple has hardly left the lectern before Joel Greenberg leaps to take his place. Greenberg is in many ways the opposite of the more reserved Schorger: a loquacious, booming-voiced man fully at ease before the crowd.

"Do I need the mic?" Greenberg hollers, and though he most certainly does not, a naysayer in the back demands he use it. He acquiesces, though I get the sense he's more comfortable working the room than remaining tethered to a microphone cord.

The white-haired, bespectacled Greenberg speaks with an air of confidence, and for good reason. He's the author of the 2014 book *A Feathered River across the Sky: The Passenger Pigeon's Flight to Extinction.* It is, perhaps, second only to Schorger's work on the species, though it's more accessible to a general audience, as is Greenberg himself.

He begins his lecture by describing a familiar scene: vast flocks of Passenger Pigeons darkening the skies—at least until the flocks diminished.

"They were killed in many ways," Greenberg explains, "torches, clubs, nets, guns, boots. Killing them was too strong a human virtue to withstand."

He moves from one PowerPoint slide to the next, eventually coming to a portion of the story I've never heard before: technology's role in the bird's undoing.

"Two technologies, in particular," Greenberg explains, "the introduction of the telegraph and the railroad."

They worked in tandem—the telegraph allowing scouts to offer reconnaissance on the flocks' positioning, while the railroad allowed hunters to dramatically increase shipping speeds, thereby expanding potential markets. The process allowed professional hunters to "kill without interruption," Greenberg explains, and was so successful in its efficiency that the hunters soon ran out of supply.

Yet the Passenger Pigeons' problems transcended technology, Greenberg continues. The birds also had a less than robust breeding pattern, one that limited each breeding pair to a single egg per nest per season. Thus, as the number of birds dwindled, so too did the breeding pairs, and as the pairs dwindled, so too did the number of eggs. In some ways, the situation illustrated the converse of the old causality dilemma: "Which came first, the chicken or the egg?" Though in this instance, we're left wondering which vanished first, and the answer is obvious: the pigeons did.

For decades the birds' numbers continued to diminish, and by the turn of the twentieth century, it was all but impossible to spot a Passenger Pigeon in the wild. These sightings became even more difficult after April 3, 1902, when the last confirmed wild Passenger Pigeon was shot in Laurel, Indiana. However, it's death hardly kept others from claiming to have spotted the birds themselves. Even sitting president Theodore Roosevelt claimed to have observed a small flock in Albemarle County, Virginia, in the spring of 1907. Despite these occasional wild sightings, within a few years' time, even the chance to see Passenger Pigeons in captivity would fade.

Such was the case on September 1, 1914, when Martha—the world's last known Passenger Pigeon—died in her cage at the Cincinnati Zoo.

"We can pinpoint the last," Greenberg stresses to the crowd. "It is very rare that we can do so with such certainty."

We have a name for the last representative of a species. We call them "endlings"—a fraternity with far too many members as it is.

Martha is a member, as is Benjamin the Tasmanian tiger, and Celia the Pyrenean ibex. And how can we forget Lonesome George, the last Pinta Island tortoise, who died in 2012 at the age of 102.

From a conservation perspective, it is indeed discouraging to read of these disappearing creatures, though the writer in me is equally disheartened by our need to invent a word for them.

You are an endling, we say of Martha or Benjamin or Celia. *You are what we've let get away.*

Yet perhaps there is an upside to bestowing them with such a distinction. By doing so, we recognize them as individuals, reminding ourselves that flocks consist of birds, each of whom possesses a heart, a pair of wings, and the homeostatic tendency to endure.

While stories of individual animals are of great interest to me, they are of little interest to nature. "Nature is little concerned with the fate of the individual," Don Eckelberry confirmed in a 1961 essay, "but there is no greater tragedy in the scheme of things than the extinction of a species."

Perhaps he's got a point. Or perhaps they're simply tragedies of scale.

I've already speculated whether a man like Francis Zirrer was himself an endangered species, though after rereading his correspondence, I wonder, too, if the man on the other end of those letters was equally rare, an endling in his own right.

Who, after all, was Bill Schorger?

In a 1993 issue of the *Passenger Pigeon*, Dr. Robert McCabe noted that his former colleague was a "difficult" man to get to know. "He was selective in his friendships," McCabe wrote. "I never heard him say he either liked or disliked anyone."

But as McCabe made clear, Schorger was far from perfect. In fact, while reading McCabe's retrospective on the man, I'm left wondering if it's supposed to serve as a tribute or a roast.

"I have not seen a photograph either candid or professional that shows [Schorger] smiling," McCabe wrote, though, in the very next line, he added that the man had a "wonderful sense of humor."

McCabe described his first encounter with Schorger during his time as a graduate student under the tutelage of Aldo Leopold. Leopold had encouraged his pupil to join a local birding club in Madison, one that claimed Schorger among its ranks.

At the start of each meeting, members would report on recent sightings, though as McCabe noted, "If a very early [bird] arrival was reported, all eyes focused on Schorger since he always challenged such observations, and the interrogation that followed was often as intimidating as it was brusk."

McCabe recalled one instance in which a "competent young ornithologist" claimed to have spotted Western Meadowlarks, a claim that Schorger disputed.

"Were the birds singing?" he demanded.

"No," the young ornithologist replied.

"Then how do you know they were Western and not Eastern Meadowlarks?" Schorger pressed.

Unintimidated, the young ornithologist offered an unmistakable description of the birds' trademark yellow throat reaching toward the bill.

"The expression on the faces of the younger members was that of a loud cheer," McCabe recalled. "A. W. merely sat down."

Yet a few lines later McCabe offered a counterweight to his rather condemning story, noting how he came to value the "important role Schorger played as the devil's advocate, guarding the integrity of our club."

Though McCabe implicated Schorger on only one observational error in the field (it involved a woodcock chick), in several instances he made mention of Schorger's personal failings, most notably Schorger's refusal to accept feedback on his writing. This became clear to McCabe after he attempted to provide Schorger a few solicited thoughts on his Passenger Pigeon book.

"I made a number of suggestions, of which all but one were minor," McCabe wrote. "When I discussed these ideas with him, he rejected them in a very hostile manner and in a way that regarded my sincere effort as less than competent."

McCabe's primary concern, however, wasn't what Schorger had written, but what he'd omitted.

"I let him know in terms not easily confused that he, who was in the best position, ought to philosophize in the summary and underscore this tragic loss of a species through avarice and greed of man."

McCabe felt his plea "fell on deaf ears."

While Schorger did, in fact, integrate a bit of the proposed language, all philosophizing was kept at a minimum. Yet even with the additions, McCabe considered Schorger's book a mostly unfeeling tome. As proof, he cited the book's innocuous and forgettable last line: "A photograph of a nest with an egg occurs in Craig.'"

Upon reading it myself, I can't help but concur with McCabe.

"There was no last word, no summing up," McCabe wrote, "it was as if the pen had run dry. The sensation to me was like watching a miner laboriously dig a shaft and just as he at last reached the mother load turned and walked away to dig another shaft in another mountain."

Schorger's ripe opportunity to appeal to readers' hearts and minds had, according to McCabe, been squandered. While Schorger's science remained spot-on, what good were the facts if few people bothered to read them?

Despite McCabe's frustrations with Schorger's occasional stubbornness, it was this same stubborn spirit that propelled Schorger as a researcher. When called upon to answer a question he'd forgotten, Schorger would "relentlessly recheck the point in a library and—no matter how trivial—report the answer a day or two later," remembered McCabe.

Though this meticulous research was hardly a chore given that the library had become a second home for him. After a full day of work at Burgess Cellulose (this was prior to his days at the university), Schorger would famously log a few additional hours at the Wisconsin State Historical Society Library, prompting one librarian to remark ("in a tone of utter despair," Schorger's former colleague Joseph Hickey recalled) that she had "moved more tons of paper for [him] than for any other ten persons in Wisconsin!"

Schorger was hardly browsing, but rather committing himself to a twenty-year project of leafing through every page of every Wisconsin newspaper printed prior to 1900. His mission: document every mention of Wisconsin's natural history, in particular, its flora and fauna.

It was a daunting undertaking, one he organized in conjunction with Aldo Leopold during a three-year stint between 1937 and 1939. Yet once the Works Progress Administration funds ran dry, Schorger continued on in what seemed a Sisyphean task, though not for him, who, according to McCabe, never tired of a "self-chosen chore."

And so he flipped page after dust-covered page in an effort to observe nature in newsprint, to unearth once more the stories that time forgot.

While Schorger contributed the most scholarly work on the Passenger Pigeon, perhaps it's Aldo Leopold's take on the species that we remember most.

On several occasions throughout the symposium, Stanley Temple makes mention of Leopold's renowned essay "On a Monument to the Pigeon," a reference often followed by a description of the monument itself.

Erected by the Wisconsin Society of Ornithology in 1947, the monument received renewed attention in May 2014 when Temple and others rededicated it in honor of the hundred-year anniversary of the birds' extinction. The monument—situated in southwest Wisconsin's Wyalusing State Park—appears modest from the pictures I've seen: a stone structure atop a cliff overlooking the Wisconsin River. Yet it's unique, Temple tells those of us in the audience, because it's "one of the original places where humans publically expressed regret" for their role in a species' extinction.

Months later, I'll chat with one of Wyalusing's retired park rangers, a man who for over twenty years watched day hikers inadvertently stumble upon the monument. He'll confirm that the monument's candid assessment of our role in the species' extinction often proved to be a powerful lesson.

"For a lot of people," the ranger tells me, "the monument is their first exposure to the bird and the story behind it. And once they hear it, they're pretty fascinated."

I suspect visitors are pretty surprised, too, upon learning that we've constructed a monument to our culpability. Though no one reading this book is personally responsible for the extinction of the Passenger Pigeon, most of us can't help but feel a pang of regret—a sentiment Leopold highlights in his essay.

As I sit in the Marquee Theater, I can't help but feel that pang myself. I try to push it aside, bury it, and instead focus on the comfort of my surroundings—a symposium that is neither a celebration of what once was nor a memorial of what won't ever be again, but an opportunity to come together and confirm that we are not alone in our sorrow and fascination.

Though our particular flock remains small, there are other flocks of folks who care just as deeply as we. People like Temple and Greenberg are making sure of it, spreading their conservation-minded message widely, just as Schorger and Leopold had for the previous generation.

None of these men were in a position to save the Passenger Pigeon, though they've done much to preserve its memory. But for Leopold, the mere memory of a bird now confined to specimen drawers and history books hardly seemed sufficient.

"Book-pigeons," Leopold wrote, "cannot dive out of a cloud to make the deer run for cover, or clap their wings in thunderous applause of mast-laden woods. Book-pigeons cannot breakfast on new-mown wheat in Minnesota, and dine on blueberries in Canada."

Two months after the symposium, on a snow-soaked January morn-ing, I decide that I, too, have had quite enough of book-pigeons.

It's time, I think, *to see what I can't for myself.*

I put down my books, pick up my keys, and drive toward the thun-derous applause.

A century after the last one's death, I strike out in search of a Pas-senger Pigeon. Or at least what's left of them—the stone monument in Wyalusing State Park, a known migration corridor for the birds. I drive south (spot an eagle, some Tree Sparrows) until I reach the park's entrance, which has not been plowed and poses a challenge for my Ford Focus. The car crawls to a halt near Long Valley Road, not far from an ice-encrusted volleyball net. The park is a freshly shaken snow globe—beautiful but desolate, not a person or pigeon anywhere.

While the symposium is partially to blame, my pilgrimage is mostly inspired by Leopold's pigeon essay, which, upon reading it for the first time, aroused within me such an unrelenting guilt that I found myself re-sorting the recycling bin three times through that week.

Maybe it wouldn't bring back any Passenger Pigeons, but I'd sleep a little easier.

How else was I to respond to Leopold's hard truth: that no human would ever again see "the onrushing phalanx of victorious birds . . . chas-ing the defeated winter from all the woods and prairies of Wisconsin."

I could have used some of their winter chasing on the day I arrive at their monument. Or almost arrive there. I don't dare drive down the accurately named Long Valley Road so I get out and walk instead. The problem, though, is that I'd been too cheap to pay for the full-day park pass, opting for the hour-long rate. Which means I have to hustle, really hustle, or I might just miss my monument.

If you've never seen a grown man sprint through the trees, binoc-ulars bouncing, I highly recommend it. That is, assuming you are not that grown man. Thankfully, save for a rabbit and a couple of deer, my tracks are the only tracks in the snow.

A few steps shy of experiencing a coronary event, I at last reach my monument. I recognize it from pictures—a miniature monolith upon which rests a plaque featuring an engraving of our departed bird. And just below, a line that will soon have me absolving myself once more in the recycling bin: "The species became extinct," it reads, "through the avarice and thoughtlessness of man."

I am still breathless, frantic, checking my watch; my time here, I know, is short. But so was the Passenger Pigeons', once we began clouding their sky with our nets and our smoke and our bullets.

From my place on the bluff, I am at last eye-level with the birds. Though there are no birds, not today.

What better reminder, I think, *of our own mortality than a sky with no wings on the wind?*

Ten minutes later, I retrace my tracks through the snow. Still, no one is anywhere—no people, no pigeons, certainly no snowplows.

I combat my solitude by imagining Schorger and Leopold making this trek long before, their necks craned in search of pigeons. And I imagine Francis Zirrer, too, in a distant bog, scanning the skies for his goshawk.

But on this day, the memory of these men does little to counteract the unsettling solemnity afforded by the forest. It feels as if I'm the last one left—a human endling—the world turned silent beneath my boots.

The muted sky is equally disconcerting, further proof of what I've long feared—that our past transgressions are coming home to roost.

The echo of the emptiness is deafening.

1. Frederick William Frohawk's painting of the Dodo (1905) featured in Lionel Walter Rothschild's *Extinct Birds: An Attempt to Unite in One Volume a Short Account of Those Birds Which Have Become Extinct in Historical Times: That Is, within the Last Six or Seven Hundreds Years: To Which Are Added a Few Which Still Exist, but Are on the Verge of Extinction* (London: Hutchinson, 1907).

2. Mark Catesby's *The Largest White-bill Woodpecker, the Willow Oak*, 1731 (later known as the Ivory-billed Woodpecker).

Psittacus Carolinensis.
The Parrot of Carolina.

3. Mark Catesby's *The Parrot of Carolina, the Cypress of America*, 1731 (later known as the Carolina Parakeet).

4. Mark Catesby's *The Pigeon of Passage, the Red Oak*, 1731 (later known as the Passenger Pigeon).

5. Photograph by J. G. Hubbard of a female Passenger Pigeon in captivity in 1898. Courtesy Wikimedia Commons.

6. "James T. Tanner standing next to a large sweet gum, May 1937." Courtesy Tensas River National Wildlife Refuge, U.S. Fish & Wildlife Service, Ivory-billed Woodpecker Records, Mss. 4171, Louisiana and Lower Mississippi Valley Collections, LSU Libraries, Baton Rouge LA.

7. "Tensas River, July 1937." Courtesy Tensas River National Wildlife Refuge, U.S. Fish & Wildlife Service, Ivory-billed Woodpecker Records, Mss. 4171, Louisiana and Lower Mississippi Valley Collections, LSU Libraries, Baton Rouge LA.

8. "Nestling ivory-billed woodpecker and J. J. Kuhn, March 6, 1938." Courtesy Tensas River National Wildlife Refuge, U.S. Fish & Wildlife Service, Ivory-billed Woodpecker Records, Mss. 4171, Louisiana and Lower Mississippi Valley Collections, LSU Libraries, Baton Rouge LA.

9. Dusky Seaside Sparrow, photograph by P. W. Sykes. Courtesy Wikimedia Commons.

10. James Newman Clark. Courtesy University of Wisconsin–Eau Claire, Special Collections and Archives.

11. (*top*) James Newman Clark Bird Museum at the University of Wisconsin–Eau Claire. Courtesy UWEC Photography/Shane Optaz.

12. (*bottom*) James Newman Clark Bird Museum. Courtesy of UWEC Photography/ Shane Optaz.

13. The author at Kissick Alkaline Bog Lake State Natural Area in search of the remains of Francis Zirrer's cabin, Hayward, Wisconsin, 2015. Courtesy of Justin Patchin.

PART III

Seeing

7

The Stunning Conclusion of the Continuing Saga of the Resurrection of the Lord God Bird

I'm Don Eckelberry and I paint birds. And that's a very curious profession. It takes years of field work to get to know birds well enough to paint them properly.
—Don Eckelberry, *Bird in the Hand, Bird in the Bush*, 1970s

After six months of searching, I stumble upon the last Ivory-billed Woodpecker America has ever known.

Though, admittedly, what I find in a file folder in Wausau, Wisconsin, hardly qualifies as an Ivory-billed Woodpecker. It isn't exactly flesh, blood, and feathers after all; rather, it's an artist's depiction of the last.

To be clear, when I use the phrase "last Ivory-billed Woodpecker" in describing what I find, I'm asking you to disregard the previously discussed alleged sightings in Arkansas in the mid-2000s.

And so, perhaps my opening hook demands a bit of clarification:

After six months of searching, I stumble upon the last *artistic depiction* of the last *confirmed* Ivory-billed Woodpecker America has ever known.

(It's a claim, I admit, with more holes than a woodpecker-filled cypress tree).

Yet on that January morning, as I drive one hundred miles due east from my home in Eau Claire to Wausau's Leigh Yawkey Woodson Art Museum, I don't expect to find much in the way of Ivory-bills. Or at least nothing I haven't seen before.

Rather, I make the drive to see what other rare birds the museum might have on display. Known internationally for its annual *Birds in Art* exhibition, the museum is a "must" for budding birders. (Especially those, like myself, who needs their birds confined to a canvas to make a proper ID.) Yet I arrive months after *Birds in Art* in order to experience an exhibition even more closely aligned with my project: *Legacy Lost & Saved: Extinct and Endangered Birds of North America.*

I jog toward the museum's glass doors at a few minutes before 8:00 a.m., bypassing the pair of snow-capped crane sculptures and a gaggle of metallic turkeys. Though the museum doesn't open to the public for another hour, my guide, Curator of Collections Jane Weinke, has agreed to offer me the early bird tour.

I ring the bell, peering inside the foyer to find a small-framed woman complete in blue sweater and gray slacks headed my way at a clip. Before unlocking the door she pauses, furrows her brow, then nods and swings it wide.

"Sorry about that," she says. "I always have to think if I have to do anything before I open up. You know, so the alarms don't go off."

"We don't want the cops coming after us," I agree.

Jane smiles, but the need for alarms is no joke. The museum, after all, houses thousands of pieces of priceless art—from Audubon originals to works from more modern wildlife masters: Roger Tory Peterson, Arthur Singer, among others. That she would unlock the doors for a stranger is a gift I hardly deserve, but it's a gift I'll treasure.

The early morning sun has just begun to seep through the various windows, warming the room and bringing a bit of the outside in. Not the subzero temperatures, mind you, but the stark stillness of Wisconsin in winter; a stillness made all the more apparent by the bird sculptures outnumbering their living brethren in the trees.

"Not a bad place to work," I say, admiring the newly constructed foyer bridging the gallery wings. "How'd you end up here?"

"I started in 1979," Jane begins. "I was a student at U W –Stevens Point, and I was kind of lost; I didn't know what I wanted to do with my life. So, I took a semester off. My parents were friends with someone on the board of directors here, and they were looking for a gardener. I said, 'I can do that.'"

"So you were into gardening?"

"Not really," she shrugs. "But this was the '70s, and the idea of riding around on a lawn mower all summer and getting a tan, well, vain as it was," she laughs, "that's what started it."

"Okay," I clarify, "so you weren't *exactly* a gardener, but you must have an interest in birds."

"Well, I had a Peterson field guide growing up," she says, "but I admit, I know almost nothing about birds. Thankfully, I have plenty of friends in the birding art world, so when I have an image I can't identify I email it to them and say, 'Tell me what the hell this is.'"

As Jane explains, her curatorial work transcends any one "type" of art; she's the curator for the museum at large, not just the curator for bird art. As such, her rise from gardener to curator—though unconventional—provided her the perfect training to develop the wide range of skills necessary to curate the museum, including how to build lasting relationships with a variety of artists.

As we walk toward the gallery, Jane offhandedly mentions one such relationship that recently led to the museum's acquisition of the artist's body of work.

"Who's that?" I ask.

"Don Eckelberry."

I stop midstep.

"*The* Don Eckelberry?" I ask. "The one who sketched America's last Ivory-billed Woodpecker?"

"Yes," she agrees, leading me into the gallery, "that's the one."

Born in 1921 in Sebring, Ohio, Donald Richard Eckelberry ("He always just went by Don," Jane informs me) spent much of his life observing and painting birds. But prior to painting them, he shot them, the result of receiving an air rifle for his thirteenth birthday. However, it didn't take long for Eckelberry to realize that paintbrushes, rather than air rifles, allowed him greater access to the birds' "life situation." Two years later he'd formed a local birding club, and within a few years' time, he enrolled at the Cleveland Institute of Art. Following the completion of his artistic training, a fortuitous meeting with National Audubon Society director John Baker led him to Louisiana, where he served briefly as a wildlife warden. And it was Baker, too, who in 1944 dispatched the young artist to the Singer Tract to sketch America's last-known representative of the species.

Though I'd never heard of Eckelberry during his lifetime, after learning of his role in the Ivory-bill's story, I do my best to make up for lost time. Yet despite the many paintings and sketches he left behind, ultimately it's a low-budget and little-known film entitled *Birds in the Hand, Birds in the Bush* that helps me to know him better. The film—which documents one of Eckelberry's 1970s trips to Trinidad—offers what his artwork cannot: a living, breathing Eckelberry captured on film.

"I'm Don Eckelberry," the film opens, "and I paint birds. And that's a very curious profession. It takes years of field work to get to know birds well enough to paint them properly."

Eckelberry speaks while seated in his home studio, the sleeves of his salmon-colored button-down rolled up past his elbows, his mustache twitching with every word. His voice takes on a grandfatherly tone—calm and affirming, thoughtful and generous of spirit.

In the film's background, I hear birds calling from elsewhere in Eckelberry's house, confirming the ambiance I'd imagined for him, one revealing a life spent *among* the birds, not just one spent painting them from afar.

Eckelberry was hardly the only wildlife painter committed to intensive fieldwork. The same was true of Owen Gromme, whose re-created art studio I find stretched before me on the far side of the gallery. While most remember Gromme for his paintings and curatorial work at the Milwaukee Public Museum, I know him best as the man who corroborated Francis Zirrer's goshawk sightings in the spring of 1934. Admittedly, I'd become so personally caught up in Gromme's interactions with Zirrer that upon viewing his re-created studio, I realize I know embarrassingly little about his artistic work.

Jane corrects this by leading me toward Gromme's easel and desk in the foreground, then toward the book- and specimen-filled shelves near the back. To my left are filing cabinets overflowing with magazine-torn photos of birds, all of which he used as references while painting. Gromme's binoculars are there, too (Tasco 7x35s), and with Jane's permission, I hold them to my eyes and peer at the extinct bird paintings on the opposite side of the gallery.

Could these be the binoculars, I wonder, *that he used to view Zirrer's goshawks?*

"So all of this was from Gromme's studio?" I ask.

"Well, with the exception of that desk," she says, nodding toward it, "that actually belonged to Eckelberry."

I ease the binoculars back into a drawer and make my way toward the desk. It's wooden, nondescript, and reminiscent of the school desks of my youth. Yet for me, an Eckelberry admirer, it's nothing short of a piece of bird art history. It might as well be Raphael's paintbrushes, Michelangelo's chisels, the quill belonging to Shakespeare.

Strange as it seems, just seeing the desk makes me feel closer to the Ivory-bill, the bird I know I'll never know fully.

"Don would sit right here," she explains, "and he had this little chair. His filing cabinet was to his left, and his paints were here on the right."

Jane's detailed knowledge is due to her occasional visits to Don and Virginia Eckelberry's nineteenth-century carriage house on Long Island, visits that began to raise red flags about the preservation of Don's work.

"They lived in this old, leaky-roofed house," she explains. "And not only that, but they kept birds, which aren't exactly neat creatures . . ."

They kept a cat, too, Jane remembers, one that only occasionally bothered with a litter box.

The combination of which threatened Eckelberry's art, and following his death in 2001, Jane committed herself to preserving his work as best she could. With Virginia's permission, the museum acquired over six thousand sketches, drawings, and paintings—including his sketches of the last Ivory-billed Woodpecker.

Though as Jane leads me through the gallery it's not Eckelberry's

Ivory-bill sketches, but his Singer Tract field notes, that are prominently displayed on the wall. They're arranged in two horizontal rows, seven pages in each.

"These are them?" I ask, positioning myself mere inches from the glass. "His original notes from 1944?"

Jane nods as I squint to read Eckelberry's poetic descriptions of the "vine draped trunks against the blue-green sky" and the "willows standing waste deep in muddy water." I read also how the "soft-shelled turtles sun on logs" and how the Barred Owl "flushes from its stream-side home."

But his notes capture more than mere backdrop, and on the page dated April 5—the day of his first sighting—Eckelberry offers nothing short of a play-by-play of his encounter.

6:33 Kent-kent—5 times and double knock-2–3
6:45 2 more double knocks . . .

I already know how this story ends, and yet I read his notes in great anticipation, my eyes running along the Ivory-bill's Morse code: *kent-kent, double-knock, kent-kent.*

I turn my attention to his notes from April 11:

About 5:30—KENT!
Double rap while walking
Through small uncut
area about 1/3 mile from
rd. Found her immediately.

I reread the phrase that was surely never uttered again—*Found her immediately.*

Following my initial viewing, I'm disheartened to learn that *Birds in the Hand, Birds in the Bush* makes no mention of Eckelberry's encounter with the Ivory-billed Woodpecker. Instead, the film focuses on Eckelberry's interactions with the birds of Trinidad: from the White-bearded Manakin, to the Palm Tanager, to the Golden-olive Woodpecker himself.

Perhaps the film comes closest to the Ivory-bill by showcasing Eckelberry's encounter with another rare bird: the Scarlet Ibis.

The grainy footage depicts Eckelberry and his wife floating down a river on a bright day, awaiting what his voiceover describes as "one of the great sights of the bird world."

As the boat turns into the mangroves, Eckelberry lifts his binoculars in a single, swift motion, thereby obscuring his face.

In a flash of red and white, a flock of ibises appears.

"It's a sight I've seen many times but never tire of," Eckelberry's voiceover remarks. "No pigment—whether on film or canvas—can do justice to that unbelievable red. There are some things in nature artists shouldn't attempt, and certainly this is one of them."

I smile at his pronouncement, though I can't help but wonder if there are ever exceptions to his rule; unique circumstances—such as Eckelberry's—in which an artist has no choice but to try.

For much of the morning, Jane guides me through the exhibition, revealing the many stories behind the art.

I nod as I scan the gallery's walls, which are filled with everything the skies aren't: Passenger Pigeons, Imperial Woodpeckers, even a Great Auk. And there are sculptures, too, such as Todd McGrain's *Carolina Parakeet* and Paul Rhymer's *Ivory-billed woodpecker*.

But there are also works featuring birds not yet lost, such as Louis Agassiz Fuertes's *Whooping Crane*, and Mary Cornish's depiction of a California condor in *The Contender*.

After perusing, I turn to Jane, ask, "What do you hope this exhibition reveals to people? Is there a conservation message?"

"I think," she begins," just by being here, seeing the artwork and reading the extended labels, it gets people thinking. I mean, a lot of times it feels like we're just preaching to the choir because the people who come here are generally bird lovers anyway. But I'm hopeful that when people see the art, they might think of birds differently."

"Art seems to approach the conservation message differently than a science report," I say.

"I think so," she agrees. "The message can seem simpler through art."

She pauses, her eyes staring deep into the nearest painting of an endangered bird.

"But no matter how simple the message," she says, "what always gets me is that every sad story is human related. It's us. And who was here first? We come in and think we're making the world better by building subdivisions and putting in roads and draining lakes and stuff. But we aren't."

She pauses, losing herself in the art once again.

"A negative message isn't going to get the word out. We need to say, 'Look at how beautiful this is,'" she says, pointing to a bird painting. "'Wouldn't you like to see these in nature?'"

She nods toward Eckelberry's framed field notes.

"What must it feel like to be the last person to ever see a species?" she asks. "Yay for you, but wouldn't you feel bad knowing that your grandchildren won't be able to have that experience?"

The answer, so obvious, doesn't even require my nod.

Jane and I weave through the labyrinthine museum, eventually arriving in a climate-controlled storage room in the bowels of the basement. The air vents hum overhead, doing their part to protect the hundreds of paintings hanging in the Storage Saver shelves on the far side of the room.

Jane walks me through the collection, opening and closing one rack after the next, revealing a startling array of bird art, paintings from the Wyeths, the Singers, even Audubon himself.

"This is one of Audubon's original oil paintings," she says. "He did the oil paintings after the original prints for *Birds in America*. It's one of eleven in the world. It's called *Pacific Loon (Black-throated Diver)*."

I lean in to observe a pair of loons peering beyond the limits of the canvas, the female at ease at the water's edge while the foregrounded male stares off to the right. I imagine his tremolo echoing across the water, a warning cry for whatever dangers may await them past the serenity of the momentary scene.

We move deeper into another storage room, and after bypassing two locked doors, we at last reach Eckelberry's inner sanctum. It's a shrine of sorts, stacks and boxes of Eckelberry's work, from tracing paper sketches to matted prints.

This, I realize, *is what a lifetime of work looks like.*

But what catches my eye is the one framed photo without a bird.

It's a black-and-white picture depicting a young Don posing alongside his wife, leaning against a too-cool car and peering away from the camera. He's wearing a crisp white shirt and a wry smile, a near-perfect James Dean lookalike.

"He was movie star handsome," Jane says, interrupting my thoughts. "And he had a presence . . . his oration . . . he just had the most amazing voice."

I nod, but my mind is elsewhere.

I wonder: *Was this photo taken before or after he sketched the Ivory-bill?*

Midway through the film, Eckelberry stations himself in his sparse Trinidadian studio and reaches for his paints.

"Watercolors are the medium for fast work," Eckelberry's voiceover explains. "When you're dealing with plants that wilt and birds that could die, speed is important."

The film goes on to show Eckelberry reaching into a wire cage to examine a live specimen, though when I hear Eckelberry speak of the importance of speed when painting "birds that could die," once more I think of his Ivory-bill.

How could I not?

Of all the birds he'd sketched and painted over the years, no bird's time was more pressing than hers. Especially when one considers that we aren't merely discussing the death of a specimen, but quite likely the death of a species itself.

As Eckelberry paints, his voiceover describes his process.

"I spend a good deal of time just going around looking at birds because it's necessary to know a bird very well if you intend to paint it properly. Only by watching any bird over and over again can one eventually learn what is typical in its behavior."

Though in the case of the Ivory-bill, this particular luxury hardly presented itself.

Instead, he made do with what he had—her—and watched as she soared through the evening air, "trumpeting in to the roost, her big wings cleaving the air in strong, direct flight," as she "alighted with one magnificent upward swoop."

There were a handful of other encounters, of course, but never enough for him to learn her "typical behavior." How could we expect him to, as he put it, "capture the essence of the species" when limited to observing a single representative?

"I have a sort of mental movie of every kind of bird I've ever seen adequately," Eckelberry's voiceover explains, "and this can be rerun through my mind at will. I can remember exact visual impressions back to the time when I first became interested in birds."

The difficulty, of course, is transferring one's "mental movie" onto the canvas for everyone to see.

Upon entering Jane's office, she directs me to several black filing cabinets on the far side of the room, numerous drawers of which are dedicated to Don Eckelberry.

"We've got just about every letter he ever wrote, and every letter ever written to him," Jane says, pointing to the manila folders containing correspondence between Eckelberry and any number of artists, editors, and friends.

Tucked into one folder are the sketches I most hoped to see: eight of them, each of which offers a new look at our long-lost girl.

I flip wide the folder, holding in my hands the last-known sketches of the last-known Ivory-billed Woodpecker in America. The sketches are rough, though they offer far more visual detail than the field notes hanging in the gallery below our feet. There is her crest, her ivory-colored beak, her wings carefully folded to her sides. In one sketch there are actually two of her; or, rather, two views, Eckelberry managing to double the species' entire population by way of a few extra pencil strokes.

Though most of his sketches depict the Ivory-bill on her roost tree, the one I admire most is her portrait, her neck sprung back in perpetual hold, as if preparing to debark a cypress tree. There is the white stripe of her neck, which, if followed, leads directly to her beak.

When Eckelberry drew the Ivory-bill she still breathed, rapped, had the good sense to fly away. On paper she remains motionless—not a blur or a flash, just an image—as if she'd willingly posed for him.

Though Eckelberry had described her "hysterical pale eyes," in this portrait all I see is calm. Or resignation, maybe, for a prophecy not yet fulfilled.

What must it have been like? I wonder. *To watch a species disappear before his eyes? And what must it have been like to be the last of her kind, offering her call only to hear the echo call back?*

As I stare at Eckelberry's sketches, my waxing poetic turns suddenly practical. I notice that in half of the sketches, including the portrait, the female's black crest is sketched red—the clear marking of a male. Which means nothing on its own, merely that Eckelberry was, perhaps, taking a bit of creative license to offer posterity a depiction of both.

Unless, I think, *it means everything.*

My conspiracy theory goes a little like this:

Well aware of the attention he'd draw by acknowledging the existence of a breeding pair, Eckelberry remained mum, instead reporting only the female, thereby protecting the privacy of the world's last chance for an egg. And maybe, deep in the hole in the roosting tree there was an egg, or two eggs, or enough eggs to keep our Lord God Bird alive awhile longer. Perhaps he kept his truth hidden in his sketches, until a decade or so after his death, when some poor fool who wanted too much to believe in the bird's resurrection suddenly found a new reason to do so.

Of course! I think, staring at the red crest aflame in the sketches stretched before me.

But . . . of course not, also.

What I need is some long-lost letter to confirm it, though when no such letter makes itself available, I make do with an unpublished Eckelberry poem instead.

Another clue, I think, reaching toward the carefully typed script.

In his untitled poem, Eckelberry wrote,

Mostly we are preserved
in life beyond our time
Glazed, pickled, set in amber
and casketed above the ground.

. . . casketed above the ground . . .
In silence, I return the poem to its place inside the folder.
What if, I think, *her echo wasn't an echo after all, but a "Hello, sweet-heart, welcome home"?*

I watch the film again and again, trying hard to properly ID the man.
Who was Eckelberry? I wonder. And would he have remained mum about a second bird spotted in a tree?
I doubt it.
"Ginny's sentimental about birds," he remarks in the film. "I'm not."
Had he spotted a second bird, surely he would have made the news public. After all, acknowledging a mate might have furthered the Audubon Society's cause—one more feathered reason to fight.
Which is my roundabout way of acknowledging that I know better than to believe my little conspiracy theory. That I know, too, the adverse effects hope can have on the heart and the head. The pair of birds I saw in Eckelberry's sketches can hardly overturn what I've long known to be true—that there was but one bird in the tract that day, and Eckelberry sketched her wondrously.
In a 2007 article in *Birding*, seventy-six-year-old Gene Laird—eldest child of Eckelberry's guide, Jesse Laird—confirmed that there was but one female in the tract in those days. Gene recalled his father urging him to keep an eye on the lone bird, which he did, right up until the day the wind and rain uprooted her roost tree, after which Gene never saw her again.
Once Eckelberry left the swamp, it was Gene's job to gather up the many sketches the artist had left behind. Just a boy then, and with no knowledge of their value, Gene simply burned them in a fire, leaving us with even fewer clues to understanding Eckelberry.
Still, seventy years later I grasp what I can from his art, his letters, his

video footage—the combination of which compels me to dream him back to life as best I can. It's not much, but it's all I have to capture his essence, to bring myself a bit closer to his "life situation."

Leaning forward on my couch, I peer at the television to find Eckelberry decked out in his safari gear—beige shirt and hat—as he whistles a birdcall into the humid Trinidadian air.

Cut to another shot as Eckelberry smokes a cigar and reaches gently for an Olive-striped Flycatcher caught in a net.

Another cut, another bird carefully studied: the Rufous-breasted Hermit, followed by the Golden-crowned Warbler, followed by the Bay-headed Tanager himself.

But of all the majestic, bird-related moments the film provides, I'm most drawn to its most understated scene: one in which Eckelberry—seemingly oblivious to the camera's presence—crouches alongside a waterfall-fed stream. From a distance, the camera captures him removing his glasses and hat, then wiping his face with his right hand as the waterfall crashes alongside him.

It is a moment both forgettable and humanizing, one that allows me to at last see this man in his native habitat, bearing his burden in peace.

On the drive home from the museum that day, I think, *Well, that's the closest I'll ever come to an Ivory-billed Woodpecker.*

But I'm wrong.

Wonderfully wrong.

And three months later I'll prove it.

8

The Christmas Count

I count each day memorable that brought me a new friend among the birds. It was an event to be recorded in detail. A creature which, up to that moment, existed for me only as a name, now became an inhabitant of my woods, a part of my life.
—Frank Chapman, *Bird-Life*, 1897

On Christmas Day 1900, thirty-six-year-old Frank Chapman—then an associate curator of ornithology and mammalogy at the American Museum of Natural History—took to the woods near his New Jersey home in search of every last bird he could find.

While the day started off cold, temperatures in Englewood rose to a seasonably warm forty-seven degrees, a wind blowing in from the southwest rocking the trees' uppermost branches. Chapman focused his eyes into those trees for much of the morning and was rewarded for his efforts, spotting a shrike, a Barred Owl, and a Red-shouldered Hawk, not to mention 150 or so Tree Sparrows, among others criss-crossing the skies. In total, Chapman identified nineteen species that Christmas; a good day of birding, to be sure, and one made all the better by the young ornithologist's successful effort to replace one holiday tradition with another.

Prior to 1900, a portion of America's hunters utilized Christmas Day to partake in what were then known as "side hunts," a pastime in which hunters divided into teams to slaughter most every animal nature had to offer. Though Christmas carols speak to the contrary, at the side hunts' conclusion, there were no partridges left in any pear trees.

Not only were these side hunts in direct opposition to the goals of the budding conservation movement, but for a man like Chapman—who admired, respected, and enjoyed nature thoroughly—the activity may have seemed indefensible. Chapman was hardly above "collecting" birds (as was the style at the time), but he did so more for study than for sport. By the turn of the twentieth century, Chapman's method of collection was already shifting from guns toward something more cerebral.

What if, he wondered one day, *we counted creatures rather than killed them?*

Chapman proposed his idea in the December 1900 issue of *Bird-Lore* magazine, for which he served as editor.

"Now *Bird-Lore* proposes a new kind of Christmas side hunt," his article explained, "in the form of a Christmas bird-census."

For many, it proved an enticing alternative, one that preserved the spirit of the hunt while preserving the lives of animals as well. In an effort to sway the more competitive hunters, Chapman encouraged participants to share their lists of sightings with *Bird-Lore*, promising to publish a portion of the results. Rather than dedicate magazine space to the traditional photos of hunters posing stoically alongside their kills, Chapman hoped the lists might sate the competitive hunters' palates.

Not that he had anything against photos. In fact, the following year Chapman would make the case for hunting with a camera. He began by noting that while the thrill of the hunt was instinctual, that same thrill could be achieved by way of photograph. Additionally, while a well-aimed gun allowed for a "certainty" of species identification, so, too, did a well-aimed camera.

"Then this desire to know definitely," he writes, "which prompts us to kill, will be gratified without the shedding of blood, and at the same time our inherent interest in animals will have been so aroused that we will recognize our kinship with them and in doing so become protectors, not destroyers."

Chapman was but one of many outdoorsmen from the era whose evolving views on hunting were linked to a newfound kinship with the natural world. And on Christmas morning 1900, more than a few took Chapman up on his call for a census rather than a hunt. As he scanned the skies, so, too did twenty-six others, their combined efforts providing bird data on twenty-five separate locations throughout the United States and Canada. In total, that first count yielded over eighteen thousand individual bird sightings representing eighty-nine individual species. Though modest in number of participants and locations, Chapman surely deemed his census a success. After all, it was the first step toward eroding an unsavory hunting practice, not to mention its usefulness as a data-gathering tool.

Despite its modest start, the popularity of the Christmas Bird Count was soon to dramatically rise. The National Audubon Society, which now sponsors the event, reports that by 1950, the 25 initial locations had increased to a whopping 403. By 2008 they had reached over 21,000. This increase in locations was directly linked to an increase in participants; while those first twenty-seven bird census takers had performed admirably, by 1950 the band had grown into a battalion forty-six hundred strong, increasing to a brigade of sixty thousand by 2008.

While these explosive numbers certainly speak to the growing popularity of birding, keep in mind that not all of these birders are seasoned experts. Christmas Counts serve as an entry point for many amateurs anxious to give birding a try alongside the pros.

Which is how I enter the scene: droopy-eyed, binocular-less, and without a clue of what is to come.

On a cold January morning, I stir to the sound of my alarm clock. It's half past 5:00 a.m., and after pulling myself into long underwear, insulated jeans, and finally, the thickest coat I own, I eventually leave the warmth of my home to slip into my freezing car.

As my breath fogs the windows I think, *Maybe it's time to find a better hobby.*

Though for me, over the past few months birding has become more than a hobby. These days, it's almost a way of life. Which isn't to say I spend hours peering into the treetops on a daily basis, but simply that I now make the effort to listen to the bird calls that surround me, to tilt my head toward the occasional flash of feathers bursting forth from the trees.

I insert the key into the ignition and listen to the battery chug before at last begrudgingly turning over. Huddled over the steering wheel, I make the teeth-chattering drive to Steve Betchkal's house and, upon arriving there, am immediately greeted by his tall silhouette in the drive.

"I thought the cold might've scared you away," Steve calls to me through the darkness.

"It's gonna take more than a balmy sixteen degrees to keep me away," I chuckle, though what I think is: *Fifteen degrees might've done it . . .*

Thankfully, Steve's Honda Insight heats up fast, and as we begin our thirty-mile drive to Durand, Wisconsin, so does our conversation.

"How were the holidays?" Steve asks. "Good trip to Indiana?"

I tell him it was a good trip, a bit exhausting, but a good trip nonetheless.

"You know," he says, taking the road's curves hard and fast in the dark, "I attended IU during my freshman year. Back in '76. The year they won the national championship."

"You only stayed for a year?"

"I got lonely," he explains. "Moved on."

"Where to?"

"Well . . . my college career is kind of silly," he admits. "It's like Goldilocks and the Three Bears."

After his stint at IU (too cold), Steve spent two trimesters at Lawrence University (too hot) before at last settling at the University of Wisconsin–La Crosse.

"It was juuuuust right," Steve says, extending his Goldilocks metaphor, "right up until I flunked out a few years later."

Eventually, Steve received his degree from my own institution, the University of Wisconsin–Eau Claire.

"You should check out my transcript," he says. "I have something like 210 credits and one degree. Something like 36 As, 5 Bs, 3 Cs, and 14 Fs."

I nod. I've known students like Steve before.

"So you did well in the classes you felt passionate about?"

"That's exactly it," Steve agrees. "And if I didn't care about it, I'd usually just skip it and write poetry, instead."

From an early age, Steve had little patience for activities he didn't deem worthwhile, though he gave himself fully to those he did.

At thirteen, while flipping through an issue of *LIFE* magazine, he stumbled upon an article on the first Earth Day, scheduled for April 22, 1970.

"And the article had a picture of the Earth Day symbol—this little green *e*—and I remember cutting it out and making my own Earth Day flag," Steve says. "I was just old enough to feel the formation of these concepts, and I was really into it."

"What was that first Earth Day like?" I ask. "Were there activities?"

"Nah, there were no such things as activities back then," Steve jokes. "People were just kind of looking around staring at each other. And I was completely looking from the outside. I was just some young kid from Racine, so I never actually met another person who said anything about Earth Day that year. But," he continues, "I remember thinking that it made sense to me to honor the earth. People like Aldo Leopold had been speaking about it for years, but the idea of incorporating it into a social movement was brand new."

And it was just the idea the environmental movement needed. While the passage of the National Environmental Policy Act of 1969 did much from a legislative perspective, Earth Day would do much for public relations. In an era of discontent, twenty million Americans had found reason to mobilize around the issue of environmental reforms, creating a spot of hope in the midst of a morally conflicted nation.

While America was finding its way into the future, so too was Steve.

He'd attended Catholic school until he was sixteen, at which point his cash-strapped parents gave him the choice to attend public school or help pay for his education. Steve chose the former. Upon enrolling in his new school, he soon found himself in an English class taught by a Mr. Barootian, a hard-nosed veteran teacher who exposed Steve to an array of philosophical texts—from the works of Hermann Hesse to Nikos Kazantzakis.

"Their books got me thinking so much," Steve recalls, "and Hesse's *Demian* really got me thinking about how the artist must forsake all else for art. I remember being sixteen and just thinking about all of this before bed. And it was like this lightbulb suddenly came on."

He pauses before continuing: "You know *Star Wars*, right?"

I nod.

"What always intrigued me about those movies was the concept of The Force. I mean sure, on one level *Star Wars* is just this goofy sci-fi movie, but The Force made it seem like more than that. To me, it sort of symbolized this connection with the universe. Earth Day was saying the same thing," he continues. "People were finally saying, 'God isn't just going to church. God is connecting with nature and connecting with systems, and having this point of view that you aren't just alone in the world doing your thing and then going off to visit God when you die.' It was beginning to dawn on people, and especially me, that heaven is *here*," he says, pounding the steering wheel. "You have to make *this place* your heaven."

I ponder his words as we sit in perfect silence, illuminated by the glow of the dash.

"Wow," I say at last. "Maybe you should've stuck it out at Catholic school. You would've made a great priest."

"Yeah," he laughs, "I've always been pretty good at sermons."

At around 6:30 Steve and I pull into the Durand Jr./Sr. High School parking lot. There's only one other vehicle there, and it's waiting for us. We park, grab our gear, then step into the early morning to meet Steve's birding buddy, Dave Linderud, a retired wildlife biologist for Wisconsin's Department of Natural Resources.

Even in the dark, I can see that Dave towers over my five-foot nine-inch frame. I extend my hand, introduce myself, thank him for having me along.

"The more the merrier," he says. "It's always more fun with a crew."

Dave offers a brief smile, returning his gloved hands into the pockets of his thin L. L. Bean jacket. I scan him from head to toe, beginning with his camouflage Cabela's cap and working down to his blue jeans and boots.

How, I wonder, *does the man retain heat?*

Shivering, I climb into the backseat of his Chevy 4x4 while Steve sits shotgun.

"This'll be fun," Dave repeats, easing his foot to the accelerator and settling in for our long morning of stop-and-go driving.

Which, for the uninitiated, is mostly what Christmas Counts are—hours spent barreling along back roads until a bird is spotted, at which point the driver squeals to a halt.

Common side effects include: whiplash, followed by more whiplash.

From my place in the backseat, it's a price I'm willing to pay. I'm just grateful Dave's the one doing the driving. After twenty-six years spent cruising these roads in his DNR car, surely no one knows them better than he. But as I soon learn, Dave knows roads beyond these roads as well.

"Saw Lars the other day," Dave says, referring to the Northern Hawk Owl that's recently taken up residence on Lars Road, just five miles south of Eau Claire.

"Yeah?" Steve asks.

Dave nods.

Over the past few weeks, Lars had become the talk of our town, at least within the birding community. In fact, excluding myself, I know of no other self-respecting birder who hasn't met Lars. On New Year's Day, even the local paper picked up on the story, complete with a photo of the thirteen-inch stripe-feathered creature perched atop his telephone pole.

The owl, while not rare, is wholly unique in this region. Given that his typical range stretches from Alaska through southern Canada, any sighting in the Lower 48 comes with a bit of hubbub. Lars is no exception. Over the past few weeks, his presence had inspired a number of midwestern birders to make the pilgrimage to meet him.

In my notebook, I add one more line to my birding bucket list (*Find Lars!!!*) as Dave drives us into the small town of Nelson, parking his truck at Beth's Twin Bluff's Cafe—the Christmas Count's meeting place.

The white café is drenched in early morning moonlight, its luminescence reflected off the snow as one birder after another begins shuffling inside. I trail Dave and Steve, listening to the tingle of the welcome bell as the smell of coffee and butter infiltrates my nose. The café's warm, inviting, and makes a pretty strong argument against returning to our frosty vehicles so we can count some birds.

But this is our task, after all, and we citizen scientists have signed up for it. After a few minutes of handshakes and small talk, the organizer distributes maps and count lists. The room is full of veteran birders—many of whom I'd met at the Chippewa Falls count—my first—a few weeks prior.

I smile as boisterous voices fill the cafe, all of them booming about birding.

"See anything good on the Durand count?" someone asks.

"Not much," replies another, "just the usual suspects."

From the far corner of the room I overhear yet another mention of Lars, and my smile widens.

What would that Hawk Owl think, I wonder, *if he knew of his celebrity status?*

I huddle alongside Steve, hopeful that his own celebrity might dim any unwanted attention toward me. "Unwanted" because when approached by a true birder, I always fear I'll be exposed as a fraud, or more accurately, an enthusiastic amateur.

My plan only half works, and after a few minutes, a kind-faced woman in her late fifties wanders over to greet me.

"Hi, there," she says. "I think we met at the Chippewa count."

"Of course," I agree, taking her hand. "How'd it go? What'd you see?"

She gives me the rundown, and I nod knowingly (or at least in a manner that gives the impression that I'm familiar with the species she's rattling off).

"And you?" she asks. "What'd you see?"

Thankfully, I'd remembered the big ones: the Bald Eagles, the Ring-necked Pheasant, the Red-tailed Hawks, and our crown jewel—the trio of Goldeneyes bobbing about in the Chippewa River.

"A respectable twenty-four species in all," I conclude, parroting Steve's phrasing verbatim.

She smiles, wishing me luck on the day ahead as she weaves back through the crowd toward her table.

I sigh, seeming to have passed the test without exposing myself.

A moment later, Steve glances up from the map of our territory.

"Ready?" he asks.

I glance out the frozen-flaked window.

We go anyway.

Dave drives us into the dawn, past the wood-dappled bluffs and the ice fishing huts as we head toward County Road KK.

Steve and I pass the time peering out the window, watching as clumps of ice fishermen prepare their holes with hand augers.

"They don't drive out on the ice yet, do they?" Steve asks.

"Nah," Dave says. "They might take a snowmobile or ATV, but they won't drive it."

We wrap around a few more bends, eventually coming to a truck parked on the right side of the road. Dave honks, tells us he knows the guy, that the man's setting muskrat traps.

As the day progresses, I'll learn that Dave knows most every person we pass. At least it seems that way. But even when he doesn't, he'll wave anyway, lifting his index finger an inch off the wheel to acknowledge the passing driver. I marvel at his knowledge of this land and its people, his ability to pinpoint property lines at fifty miles per hour while simultaneously offering information on the rotation of crops. He's a man who can point you to the best trap lines and fishing holes, though modest and soft-spoken as he is, he never offers more than he's asked.

Which prompts me to do a lot of asking.

"What kind of tree is that?" I ask regularly. "What kind of cow?"

Dave knows, and though he knows his birds, too, Steve remains our primary go-to on all things ornithological.

Meanwhile, I pull my weight by identifying every fake bird in the tri-county region, the excitement rising in my throat again and again as I spot several wood-carved owls propped atop telephone poles, not to mention a few paint-chipped Pileateds fastened to fence posts.

I point out each with gusto, prompting Steve to correct my errors again and again.

"Oh, right," I always repeat, returning Steve's backup binoculars to my chest. "I thought that was a little too easy."

Eventually, we spot live birds, too, beginning with the Dark-eyed Juncos, then a starling, then a Downy half hidden in a pine. Steve scans the landscape, rattling off identifications with ease. But he takes time to teach me, too, reminding me where and how to look.

"Keep your eyes out for blobs," Steve says, nodding to the tree line. "Sometimes it'll just be a leaf bird, but often you'll get a hawk."

It wasn't until birding with Steve that I began to understand the importance of identifying birds beyond the birds themselves. Yes, a bird's shape, size, and song all serve as important identification clues, but so are a bird's habitat, its migratory patterns, as well as the season in which one finds himself birding. All of these factors contribute to Steve's holistic approach to identification, one in which the best guess is often the most obvious one. If a bird species fits the habitat, the season, the song, the shape, and the size, then Steve can be confident in his ID. It's an approach that keeps birders honest, a checks and balances for the ornithological world.

And it's what keeps people like me from shouting, "Ivory-billed Woodpecker!" every time I spot a paint-chipped Pileated on a fence post.

Our first hour goes mostly as expected: a preponderance of Rock Pigeons, alongside the occasional nuthatch, crow, and jay.

But then, just as boredom threatens, we're greeted by a flurry of unexpected birds.

"Horned Larks!" Steve shouts.

Dave whips us to the side of the road as we reach for our binoculars.

For an instant, we catch the brief flash of fifteen or so Horned Larks, their dark face masks blurring past us as they flutter into the brush. They are there and then they aren't, all of it occurring so fast that I barely have time to form a memory of what I've seen.

And then, a few minutes later, an even more puzzling creature appears, one, thankfully, willing to loiter.

"Slow down, Dave," Steve says, reaching for his binoculars. "I want to check out the blob in that tree . . ."

I mimic Steve's moves, fitting binoculars to my eyes and peering into the treetops.

It's a big blob, I know that much, and after working through my checklist (habitat, season, size, shape, song) I place my money on a Red-tailed Hawk.

Steve seems less sure.

"It's got this strange yellow streaking on its head," he says, stumped, as we exit the truck and begin fitting the scope to his tripod. "Let me just focus in here."

He squints through the eyehole and immediately solves the mystery.

"Oh!" he cries with a slight chuckle. "It's a Golden Eagle!"

The eagle's unusual coloring had momentarily thrown him, though after paging through his spine-cracked Sibley's, Steve confirms that we are, indeed, observing an immature Golden.

We take turns peering through the scope, my left eye staring at the back of the eagle's plumage while my right eye waters from the cold.

It's my first Golden Eagle, a species that's hardly threatened, though nonetheless thrilling to see. The eagle shakes its feathers, adjusts itself on the branch, and then, as Dave and I step back from the scope Steve says, "Oh, look, a Bald Eagle up and to the left."

Sure enough, a Bald Eagle has encroached upon the Golden's range.

And if that wasn't enough, just to the right, a quartet of Wild Turkeys simultaneously bobs into view.

I react physically, my knees turned to jelly as I observe the resplendent variety of birds just ahead of me. It's not the birds themselves that move me, but that they appear wholly unaware of their shared space, equally disconnected from each other as well as us. From our panoramic vantage point, Steve, Dave, and I serve as witnesses to the unscripted scene, one in which predators and prey unknowingly mingle alongside one another along the near-leafless tree line.

For fifteen minutes, we humans stand on the side of the road munching Goldfish crackers as the scene plays out before us.

Then, as quickly as it began, the scene ends.

The turkeys bob into hiding, the eagles roost, and we, too, return to our natural surroundings, embraced by the warmth of the truck.

In his 1895 work *Handbook of Birds of Eastern North America*, Frank Chapman writes of birds' "fourfold relation to man." He writes of their economic value, their aesthetic value, as well as their relationship to science. Though of most interest to me is Chapman's focus on their "mythological or symbolic" relationship to humankind, the power we've endowed in their stories.

Though no augur myself, this hardly keeps me from imbuing each avian encounter with meaning. Some snowy evenings while walking home from work, I march up the hill desperate for a bird or an owl to give me some sign, and sometimes—when I'm lucky—one does. Other times my encounters are a bit more personal, though the message a bit harder to read.

Such was the case a few years back when, after a full day of teaching, I began my bike ride home through the rain. Along the way I spotted an enormous shadow crouched in the center of the bike path. I pulled to the side, aimed my bike light toward it, and was startled to face the fiery eyes of a Bald Eagle unwilling to budge.

There was no getting around it, though I tried—avoiding eye contact, keeping my head low, and wheeling my bike along the outer edge of the path. The eagle held firm, stretching wide her six-foot wings. It goes without saying that I'd never seen a Bald Eagle quite like that before: frantic, anxious, and stubbornly situated an arm's length away.

Eventually my presence was too much for her, our stalemate coming to its close as she hopped down the valley before taking flight toward the icy river. By bike light I watched her soar—not majestically, but in a manner that suggested she was injured. One of her wings failed to function properly, and I watched, horrified, as her body sank nearer and nearer to the water. Soon she was in the water, nothing left of her but a white head bobbing atop the coffee-colored river.

I prayed to every God I knew, watching her plight through half-closed eyes as she swam toward the far side of the shore. From a hundred yards away I could still see her tromping near the bare-limbed trees, angrily, it seemed, at the inconvenience I'd caused her.

I pedaled home as fast as I could and called the DNR.

"A Bald Eagle," I said breathlessly. "She's injured. On the far side of the Chippewa River."

The man on the phone informed me that they didn't "handle" that sort of thing.

"You don't handle Bald Eagles?" I asked incredulously.

"No, sir."

"Well, fine," I cried, my voice cracking, "then I guess she'll just . . . die!"

Slamming down the phone, I collapsed into the nearest chair.

Why do birds even bother with us, I wondered, *when we refuse to be bothered by them?*

Less than an hour after our eagle and turkey sightings, we're rewarded yet again.

"On the right!" Steve cries. "Pull to the right."

Dave does, at which point I see what Steve sees: two dozen or so Snow Buntings, all of which float like flakes on the wind. The males and females merge in midflight, the former sporting black feathers among their otherwise white plumage, while the latter display bits of brown and black running toward their wing tips.

Dave puts the truck in park, at which point our trio tromps into the snow-encrusted field. My boots sink five inches deep as we start toward a shallow valley, cutting through the remains of broken cornstalks en route toward our birds.

We two-time it through the field, though after making it fifty or so yards, the birds appear to be nowhere.

"Where'd they go?" Steve asks, scanning the landscape.

Dumbfounded silence.

"Did anyone see them fly toward the woods?" Steve asks.

Dave and I scratch our heads, shrug our shoulders, and wonder how birds as abundant as Snow Buntings still manage to disappear before our eyes.

We conclude our count with a celebratory meal at the Nelson Cheese Factory, a one-hundred-year-old former—you guessed it—cheese factory that now serves as a sandwich shop and market. We strip off our gear as we slip inside, past the wine room and the coolers of cheese until arriving at a pair of hanging chalkboards overflowing with menu items. After much deliberation, Dave and I go with Betty's Beef ("roast beef, provolone, sautéed onion, lettuce, tomato, with special sauce and Italian dressing; French roll") while Steve tries the cold hero ("salami, ham, provolone, lettuce, tomato, onion, green pepper, special sauce and Italian dressing on French roll").

It feels like we've earned it, and perhaps we have. After all, spotting 886 birds representing twenty-five species seems like a good day's work.

"Respectable," Steve had confirmed after tallying our count during the drive to Nelson's. "Twenty-five's respectable."

It isn't "over-the-moon" good (not "I-just-spotted-an-Ivory-billed-Woodpecker" good), but for a guy like me whose heart still flutters for every chickadee, our count seems a whole lot more than "respectable."

Though I've never before entered the Nelson Cheese Factory, its reputation precedes it; mostly due to Steve, who annually treats himself to a sandwich there at the conclusion of a successful count. Leading up to the Nelson count, Steve had twice told me the tale of his and his sons' dining experience there following a count a few years prior. How one of his sons had glanced up from his sandwich to spot what appeared to be a rough-and-tumble motorcycle gang swaggering through the doors.

Only they weren't a gang—they were birders—at which point Steve's son gasped, "Birders are fierce!"

After completing my first season of Christmas Counts, I've come to the same conclusion.

Birders *are* fierce, or they have the potential to be. Not in the brass-knuckled biker gang sense, but in their willingness to rise at dawn, leave the warmth of their beds, and strike off into the wilderness.

Their reward: birds, and often lots of them.

But for me, the reward is the journey, the chance to slough off the worries of the modern world long enough to stir the dying ember within, the spark that ties us to our ancestral past—to a time when "wilderness" was just another word for "home."

The day following the Nelson Christmas Count, I dedicate my Sunday afternoon to returning to the wilderness. Or rather, to the suburban wilderness just off of Highway 93, veering toward a neighborhood to pay my respects to Lars. I weave deeper down those streets, eventually pulling onto Lars Road—the owl's namesake—where a crowd fifteen or so strong confirms I'm in the right place.

Lars's fan club is a committed bunch—men and women mostly from Minnesota who made the drive and braved the temperatures to spend a bit of time with our owl of the hour. I suit up to join them, pressing my hands to the heater for one last moment of warmth before exiting the van and crunching down the road toward the others. A part of me (the sane part) wants nothing more than to turn back toward the van, yet even I'm beginning to understand the momentousness of the occasion; that we have been blessed with a rare guest, and that the least we can do is welcome him.

Moments later, I take my place alongside a woman buried inside a parka.

"How long you been out here?" I ask.

"Oh, since around one or so," she says.

I check my watch; it's nearing 4:00 p.m.

For fifteen minutes I infiltrate their group, enjoying a bit of birding fellowship among the friendly strangers. In unison, we aim our binoculars toward the tree, watching with great admiration as Lars does a whole lot of . . . nothing.

That is, until he does something—making a brief dart from one side of the road to the other, trading one pine tree for the next. The crowd issues a half-frozen whisper—"There he goes!"—as we redirect binoculars toward his new locale.

We avert our eyes from our owl just long enough to bask in our accomplishment. Though, of course, we ourselves have accomplished nothing, not really, other than enduring the cold. Yet for a moment, we allow ourselves to grin goofily at one another, to bite the insides of our half-frozen cheeks in a show of restraint for our shared enthusiasm.

I wonder if Frank Chapman felt this same ebullience on Christmas Day 1900, if he, too, had grinned goofily as he spotted his shrike, his Barred Owl, his Red-shouldered Hawk, proud of having spared the lives of so many birds by encouraging hunters to spare their bullets.

One hundred and fifteen years removed from that first Christmas Count, Chapman's contribution is more apparent than ever. Here we are—human icicles—shivering in unison for a chance to see an owl.

Not to shoot him, but to *see* him: to count him and give him a name.

When I can't stand the cold any longer I retreat home, though I return to Lars's tree two days later.

Then two days after that.

And the day after that.

And the day after.

Lars—my gift, my omen, my messenger—always faithfully awaits my return.

What is it? I wonder one evening as I stand at his tree. *What is it you want me to know?*

9

The Ghost of the Goshawk

What people don't understand is that extinction is always about us. What happened to the Passenger Pigeon starts the narrative for us. How many warning signs do we need?
—Paula Holahan, curator of mammals and birds, University of Wisconsin–Madison, 2015

By 1935, a year into Francis Zirrer and Bill Schorger's correspondence, Zirrer became determined to find his friend a fitting gift.

"It was my wish last winter to procure something unusual for you," Zirrer wrote. "So I am sending you one of our baby [goshawks]."

Under other circumstances, the gift of a dead goshawk might have seemed odd, though given Schorger's insatiable interest in the region's flora and fauna, Zirrer likely believed the gift an appropriate tribute for a man he greatly admired.

Schorger responded with a generous thank-you note, though privately was said to have been less than thrilled by the gift.

Given the birds' extreme rarity in the region, the gift of a goshawk

138

indeed seemed a regrettable choice, not only for Schorger, but likely for Zirrer, too. Killing an animal of such majesty, after all, was not something the hermit took lightly.

"It pleases me to know that you are satisfied with it," Zirrer replied to his friend, "as I dislike to destroy such a fine creature, unless there is a perfectly good reason to do so."

Though "friendship" hardly qualified as a "perfectly good reason," ultimately, it proved reason enough for Zirrer to lift his gun and fire.

At a loss for what to do with his "gift," Schorger donated the goshawk specimen to the University of Wisconsin's Zoological Museum, which is what brings me to the fourth floor of the L. E. Noland Zoology Building nearly eighty years later.

I arrive on a subzero February morning, infiltrating the pack of parka-clad students as I move from parking garage to zoology building. I'm grateful for my polar fleece, my thermal linings, as well as a host of other weather-resistant accouterments, the likes of which Francis Zirrer could never have dreamed. In his era, Zirrer had no choice but to spend days like today huddled in his unheated cabin, tossing a few logs on the fire and watching as the natural world froze beyond his windows.

Thankfully, my own journey into the natural world is soon to lead me back indoors.

Upon first hearing of Zirrer's gift of a goshawk, I'd asked myself, *Whatever became of it?* I'd read it still resided in Madison, and to confirm the rumor, I emailed Paula Holahan, the University of Wisconsin's curator of mammals and birds.

In my emailed plea I explained my interest in Schorger and Zirrer, as well as the rare Wisconsin bird that linked them together.

"Is there any way to know if this specimen still exists?" I inquired.

A few days later, Paula replied to confirm that the goshawk specimen in question did, in fact, still exist; moreover, she was happy to show it to me.

Which was all the motivation I needed to hop in the car and make the three-hour drive southeast to Madison.

I warm up by marching up four flights of stairs, then loiter outside Paula's office door until being greeted by the curator herself.

"Hi," she says, "you're the guy interested in the goshawk."

"Very interested," I admit.

Though, of course, my interest extends well beyond the specimen itself. What I'm after, truthfully, is tangible proof of Schorger and Zirrer's relationship beyond their letters, something that better embodies their shared passion for the natural world. Thankfully, Paula has agreed to serve as my guide, leading me through the narrow hallways of the zoology building until arriving at a locked door in the building's interior.

"Here we are," she says, inserting a key into the door, "the collections room."

We step inside, at which point we are outnumbered by a seemingly endless array of long-dead specimens. Directly ahead of us, hundreds of birds and waterfowl stand cloaked beneath translucent sheets, their webbed feet my only clue to identification. Just beyond them are rows upon rows of metal cabinets, the contents of which remain equally mysterious.

"This is the most secure room we have," Paula tells me, "because of the value of the specimens housed."

"Like what?" I ask.

"Oh, we have Passenger Pigeons," she says nonchalantly, "but we also have a lot of wolves, tigers, things people might try to sell on the black market. Some of these specimens were actually confiscated by the DNR or the U.S. Fish and Wildlife Service," she tells me. "And they turn them over to us."

"So you're the sentinel," I say. "You protect the animals *after* death."

"That's one way of looking at it," she agrees.

But as I soon learn, Paula's interested in protecting them *before* death as well, though when the opportunity fails to present itself, she makes do with the dead, using specimens to educate others.

Which is good news for me, since I have questions and am in need of an education.

Obviously, I want to know the names of every last bird in the room, but I'm equally interested in the backstory of the baby black bear stationed on the rolling cart just ahead of me, not to mention that of the Dall sheep and the feral goat, both of whose heads are mounted on the wall.

But before my peripheral questions begin to leave my mouth, Paula reminds me of my mission, leading me toward the case containing our goshawk.

"I think this is the one," she says, pulling the drawer to reveal a row of goshawks, inadvertent body doubles that make it difficult to find the one we're after.

She scans their tags before reaching for one buried a few birds deep.

"Here it is," she says. "Schorger's juvenile."

I'd long thought of it as "Zirrer's juvenile," though indeed, the gift was given to Schorger, which technically makes it his. Though now I am the one receiving it, a specimen that at last makes the men real to me. This is the very bird, after all, that Zirrer sighted, shot, and finally, sent to his pen pal 250 miles away. And it's the bird that Schorger is said to have regretted receiving, the cause of a momentary, one-sided rift between friends. Aside from the letters, it is one of the few items to have passed between them, a bird meant to serve as a gift of goodwill, though the outcome didn't match the intent.

"Yup. This is Schorger's tag," Paula confirms, reading the tiny script scrawled on the inch of paper dangling from the bird's leg. I lean closer to read the description for myself: "Shot at nest from Francis Zirrer."

The bird's death date is recorded just below: June 16, 1935.

In his letter accompanying the specimen, Zirrer recounted the details of the bird's death: how the goshawk ("about 43 days old") had been roosting in a branch about seventy feet above the ground when Zirrer aimed his .22 and fired.

Beak to feet, the bird measures in at around a foot or so, its circumference that of a summer sausage festooned with feathers. Its chest, though mostly white, is dappled with dashes of brown, while its eyes—long since replaced with cotton balls—imbue the creature with an eternal blank stare.

After careful inspection, I conclude that it is indeed an ordinary specimen of a twentieth-century juvenile goshawk, unremarkable in its physical features, though highly remarkable (at least to me) given the story of how it ended up in the drawer.

Paula places the specimen on a table not far from the black bear on the cart. I snap a few pictures and then, with Paula's permission, gently stroke that dead bird's feathers.

While doing so, I can't help but think of the people who've held it before. Such as Zirrer, who plucked the bird's body from the damp ground eighty years prior, and Schorger, who opened the mail soon after to find himself the recipient of an unexpected gift.

And finally, me; the outsider whose obsession with Zirrer and Schorger's letters ultimately led me to this place, this bird, in an attempt to better understand men whose way of life, for different reasons, was as rare as the goshawk itself. One took to the woods, the other to the library, but both seemed to find what they were looking for.

As I stare into its cotton eyes, it's hard for me to remember how this project—ostensibly on extinct birds—took a human turn upon my learning of these men. Undoubtedly, my interest in them was inspired, in part, by what they represented as individuals. While Zirrer provided proof that the twentieth century still allowed for a man to opt out of the world, Schorger provided a somewhat contradictory message: that a man needn't do so in order to appreciate nature fully.

Simply put, Schorger confirmed that there was more than one way to crack a nut, spot a bird, and be both wild and tame. For folks like myself, unwilling to opt out of the world altogether, Schorger paved another path: one in which we could be *in* the world and *of* the world simultaneously, observer and participant all at once. As both men demonstrated, our brethren—be they feathered, furred, or finned— are worth knowing. And these days, we must make a greater effort to know them; either that, or risk never knowing them at all.

Paula's interest in flora and fauna began at an early age, though her introduction to museum curating didn't occur until many years later, during her time as an undergraduate at California's Humboldt State University. Quite by chance, her campus job placed her in the university's museum; a work environment she never quite left.

"I fell in love with it," she says simply, her eyes drifting across the collections room. "And I think that's what happens to a lot of people. They stumble into a museum and then feel totally at home."

"Not a bad home," I agree.

(That is, assuming you enjoy being surrounded by thousands of dead animals.)

"Mostly, though, I love the variety of the work," she continues. "I get to interact with students, researchers, and then there's always the detective work . . ."

"Detective work?" I ask, my interest piqued.

"Oh, there's lots of detective work," she agrees. "People are always bringing in random bones and feathers, and it's my job to identify them. Sometimes state and federal agencies will bring something in, but other times it's just people off the street who find something in their backyard or while hiking in the woods."

"And you just . . . identify whatever comes in?"

"Sometimes," she says. "And we can learn a lot from what people bring. That elk skull and antlers, for instance," she says, pointing to a gargantuan bit of bone hanging directly above us, "that was pulled from Lake Wingra. And elk haven't lived in this region of Wisconsin since the 1850s. They were extirpated. So we know that this particular elk skull is likely prior to that date."

It's an interesting bit of information, though I wonder what it means beyond the context of the fact itself. I wonder what it *all* means, actually; what role collections such as this have on current research. I wonder also how, in a time of ever-increasing budgetary constraints, people like Paula argue the benefits of preserving natural history to those beyond the collections rooms.

I ask her point-blank: "So why does it all matter?"

Paula's smile wilts into a perfect horizontal line.

"I mean, *I* know it matters," I clarify, "it matters to me. But what do you tell people who don't understand, people who ask why we keep specimens, why we have museums. What do you tell them these things do for our future?"

"Well for one, we're a storehouse for natural history," she explains.

"We have specimens here that go back to the 1840s. Some of them were collected in the first biological surveys across the United States. Back then nobody even knew what was out there. But our function," she continues, "is to take these specimens and keep them in perpetuity. We do it so people like you can study them. When many of our specimens were collected, it was purely for biological inventory, but today they're being used for things nobody back then could have dreamed of."

She nods toward the egg drawers to my right.

"Take the eggs," she says. "Researchers used our eggs to help prove that DDT was thinning modern eggshells. Our collection played an integral role in helping to get the pesticide banned. And that's just one example of how something here was used. People use museum specimens across the country to study chemical deposition in skins over time. We can compare a skin from today to one preserved a hundred years ago and have a much better sense of the chemical pollutants now found in the environment."

"So specimens serve as a point of comparison?" I ask.

"Exactly. They help us better understand changes over time."

"And your job isn't just to preserve the past," I continue, "but to use the past as a means to preserve the future?"

She pauses, considers it.

"Yeah," she agrees. "You could look at it that way. I mean there's just so much to be learned from museum specimens. And we have no idea what techniques will be available to us to learn even more in the future."

As I stare across the collections room, I suddenly realize another reason why it matters.

"All of this," I say, nodding first to the drawers, then the cabinets, then the specimens, "it's for us, isn't it? We're trying to look out for our own future."

Paula nods solemnly.

"If nothing else is sustainable here," she says, "then neither are we."

Our tour continues from one drawer to the next as Paula introduces me to animals I may never see again. We begin with the tiger, then the wolves, then on to the Emperor Penguin the size of a small child.

My eyes grow as Paula pulls drawer after drawer, eventually leading me to a row of South American Tanagers, among other birds from the region. Their feathers appear velvet, the maroons and cerulean blues still vibrant after all these years.

Steve Betchkal would love this, I think, as would Don Eckelberry, Francis Zirrer, Bill Schorger, Aldo Leopold, James Tanner, Frank Chapman, and so many others.

I imagine these men would appreciate these skins not only for their aesthetic qualities, but for the stories behind the specimens themselves. As Zirrer and Schorger's goshawk has proven to me, there are always stories behind the skins, and when we bother to look, people behind those stories. And here in Madison's collections room, more than a few stories point back to Bill Schorger.

"In your email you mentioned wanting to have a look at Schorger's cougar, isn't that right?" Paula asks.

I most certainly had; it had been part of my smorgasbord request list aimed at getting me as much time as possible inside the collections room.

"Well," Paula says, pulling wide the metal doors and pointing to a pile of fur, "here he is."

I'd first read about Wisconsin's first preserved mountain lion (or cougar, as it's known regionally) while reading Robert McCabe's assessment of his former colleague Bill Schorger. According to McCabe, the creature had been killed in Appleton in 1857, when a farmer lost a colt near Ballard Road. Upon his retrieval efforts, farmer and feline came face-to-face, a standoff that ended with a bullet.

The mountain lion's postlife story grows more complicated from there, including a stint in the biology building at Lawrence College, followed by some time on a trash heap, until eventually, the taxidermied specimen was salvaged and displayed as a bit of kitsch in a northern Wisconsin bar.

Which is where Schorger enters the scene.

Upon learning of the mountain lion's less than ideal "habitat," Schorger took matters into his own hands. As legend has it, he drove to the bar, opened his wallet wide, then left that place with a mountain lion in tow.

Who can say for certain if the lion sat shotgun that day, though I hope so. And he might've, because at last he had a keeper who cared for him. I like to imagine Schorger bear-hugging his newly acquired lion all the way to the car, gently buckling him in as the barflies watched. Indeed, it makes for a wonderful story, though these details are lost to history.

What we do know is that as a result of that specimen's postlife locales, the skin was in need of repair. And in order to repair him, Schorger stripped the skin from the manikin, reducing that once mighty lion back to skin and skull. Upon completing the repairs, he gave the lion a final home right here on the fourth floor of the Zoology Department.

Entranced, I stroke the mountain lion's 158-year-old fur. Even knowing the story as I do, it's hard to imagine that this is the skin that once shrouded the animal that met his fate on Ballard Road; the one who was tossed on a trash heap, displayed in a bar, before being rescued by a man who hoped to save what he could.

But as Paula explains, the mountain lion's remains make for more than a compelling story.

"Researchers have used tissue scrapings from this skull to check the genetic variably of mountain lions," Paula explains. "Since they were extirpated so early on, there are few eastern mountain lions in museum collections."

Which is why Schorger's seemingly emotionally driven rescue mission ultimately proved important to science: it provided modern scholars a reference point into the mountain lion's past.

During graduate school in California, Paula, too, searched for specimens, traversing mountain ranges throughout the west alongside her advisor, climbing upwards of eight thousand feet to study the animal inhabitants of that altitude.

"It wasn't easy," she remarks, "but at least we got there in a four-wheel-drive truck. I often think back to those original guys who went out there on horseback all those years before. These people would ride for days and weeks at a time collecting specimens. They could be in a blizzard or a 110-degree heat, and regardless, they'd be out there making study skins."

"What motivated them?" I ask, then rephrase: "Or what motivated you?"

"It's love of nature," she says simply. "When you're out on a mountaintop under the stars, you can't help but feel like it's just you out there. There was a time while sitting in a camp chair when suddenly a weasel ran out and looked at me from six feet away. It had no fear of me. It had experienced so little human contact that it didn't even know it was supposed to have been afraid."

These days, species seemed to have wised up, at least enough to give us the widest berth possible. Which is disheartening, sure, but mostly because it reinforces the idea that our relationship with nature has changed. Which is not to say that a Garden-of-Eden-esque relationship ever existed between us. Indeed, we have long competed for resources, though perhaps "compete" is too strong a word given the inevitable outcome. We humans have a history of taking what we need, consuming what we can, and often doing so with impunity. My problem isn't so much with the taking, but the impunity.

Genesis tells us that humans were granted "dominion" over animals, which—depending on how you interpret the word "dominion"—can take on many meanings. Though after speaking with religious scholars, I'm inclined to believe that "dominion" has more to do with caregiving than consumption, that God bestowed on us a duty to protect his animals rather than a rubber stamp to do with them as we please.

We were not given impunity, but a cautionary tale.

I can't help but think of the Bible stories of my youth, Noah's Ark, in particular. How as punishment for humankind's wickedness, God tasked Noah with saving representatives from animal species and allowing much of humankind to wash away. How he sent a deluge to do the dirty work for him, thereby allowing Noah to restart the world.

As I stand in that collections room, a Passenger Pigeon specimen roosting nearby, I wonder what passes as wickedness today. I wonder, too, if we've already sealed our fate, not with a vindictive God, but with a climate in crisis, one that offers us few life rafts and fewer arks.

Paula stares glassy-eyed at the row of dead birds stretched before her.

"I've seen estimates for how many species go extinct on an almost daily basis," Paula says. "A lot of them are microbes, so people think, *Well it's just a microbe. What difference does it make?* Well, that microbe might make a lot of difference. It might be the cure for cancer."

Though Paula admits that the "human-use" argument might not be the best philosophical reason for taking an interest in dwindling species, it often serves as the most effective strategy to convey information on ecological problems to those beyond the field.

"Humans are always interested in how to make money on a resource," Paula says, "and that's often more important to people than simply preserving a species for the sake of its intrinsic value."

She opens her mouth, pausing as she reconsiders her words.

"But . . . beyond all of that, we simply have no right. We have no right to make anything extinct. What people don't understand is that extinction is always about us," Paula says. "What happened to the Passenger Pigeon begins our own narrative. How many more warning signs do we need?"

After reading his letters and examining his goshawk, I assume I've come as close to Francis Zirrer as I'll ever get. But in an effort to get a little closer, I turn once more to the world's leading expert on Zirrer (read: the only other person who's written of the man at length) in the hopes that he might have something to add.

The phone rings once, twice, and at last, Sumner Matteson picks up the line. Having dedicated his career to serving as a conservation biologist for what is now the Wisconsin DNR's Bureau of Natural Heritage Conservation, it comes as no surprise that he, too, felt compelled to learn more about Zirrer's life in the woods. While Zirrer's letters had offered me insight into the man himself, Sumner's work proved invaluable in helping me understand Zirrer within the context of his time.

We begin by discussing Schorger's goshawk (I tell him about my recent adventures with Paula) and then I ask, "So what made Zirrer do it? Killing that bird seemed so out of character."

"The thinking," Sumner begins, "and this is something that was really prevalent in the nineteenth century and the early part of the twentieth, was that the only way we could really study birds was to have them in hand. That was the predominant mode of operation for naturalists of the time."

And so, while Zirrer's shoot-to-study approach might have been at odds with some of his philosophical leanings, it was very much in line with the protocol of the era. Though as Sumner makes clear, this particular practice was changing, in part because of the passage of the 1918 Migratory Bird Treaty Act, but also due to a cultural shift.

"In the thirties and forties and fifties the growing popularity of Roger Tory Peterson's field guides—as well as the use of binoculars—made it so you didn't have to collect the specimens," Sumner explains.

But there was another advancement to consider as well—the camera, which, for Frank Chapman, provided the same scientific "certainty" of identification without the bloodletting. Despite the addition of field guides, binoculars, and cameras, many curators continued to obtain specimens, which could then be added to museum collections.

Sumner speculates that Zirrer killed the goshawk not for any collection purposes, but simply in an attempt to impress Schorger.

"Schorger and Zirrer had a mentor/mentee relationship," Sumner explains. "I think Zirrer idolized him. He was touched that someone of Schorger's stature would bother to take the time to communicate with him. As for Schorger," he continues, "he recognized that Zirrer was really a unique observer of nature. It wasn't just that he was a keen observer, but that he was an outstanding writer, too."

Of course, Zirrer would never have credited himself with such skills. Rather, he believed himself to be a subpar writer at best, and though he recorded his observations with great diligence, he never claimed to be particularly good at it.

After our careful study of Zirrer's letters and articles, Sumner and I arrive at the same conclusion: though Zirrer was a man uniquely suited for his task, his shortcoming was his inability to recognize his gifts. If Schorger hadn't encouraged him to publish his works, it's unlikely Zirrer would have done so. While Schorger's personal contributions to Wisconsin's natural history are numerous and well documented, perhaps the contribution most overlooked was his effort to ensure the longevity of Zirrer's contributions.

"I think if there's an irony to all of this," Sumner says, "it's that individuals such as Zirrer often undervalue what it is they contributed, generally because of a poor self-image. These people often tended to be reclusive, so many never even know what they are capable of."

And in Sumner's opinion, Zirrer had been capable of quite a lot.

"Through his letters to Schorger we learned that he was keeping notes and written observations of what he was seeing, and for me, that really underscores how important it is to keep records of the natural world. It's the only way we can chronicle what we have, and it's the foundation to determine what we can do to save threatened areas."

Consciously or not, Zirrer was an early advocate for conservation—a lesser-known Leopold who lived just a few hundred miles from his better-known contemporary.

"Without Zirrer we would be somewhat less informed on what's out there," Sumner says, "but also, we would have less of an attachment to the natural landscape."

While conservation biologists might feel otherwise, the writer in me most appreciates Zirrer's latter contribution—a contribution Leopold offered himself. While both men's observations proved to be of scientific importance, for me, it's their writing style that leaves the most lasting impression, specifically, their ability to tap into the natural world by way of vivid and memorable prose.

Much has been written on Leopold's writing, but little has been written on Zirrer's.

Yet it's a mistake to take Zirrer's limited exposure as proof of his limited contributions. To my mind, his under-the-radar status makes him all the more valuable, a hidden gem whose work is worthy of our wonderment.

How could readers not be spellbound by Zirrer's prose, whose precision borders on the poetic? Of the raven, he wrote that there was "no more impressive sight" in northern Wisconsin than a flock "flying with slow, steady, regular wing beats just above the tree tops." Though over half a century removed from that scene, the image still pricks the goose bumps on my arms. And my goose bumps only intensify upon reading Zirrer's later description of these birds, whose "deathly silence" startled him as they appeared "from nowhere" and vanished "before one finds time to think it over."

Sumner's scholarly work on Zirrer confirms his own admiration for the natural world, though he struggles to see any other similarities between himself and the hermit.

"I just don't think of myself in those terms," he says. "Though maybe," he admits a moment later, "that's similar to Zirrer, too."

For my own part, I can't help but hear echoes of Zirrer resonating in Sumner's words. Though they represent different chapters in Wisconsin's natural history story, both men have done much to preserve that story in full. While Zirrer's entrance into the natural world remains unclear, Sumner can pinpoint the exact experiences that propelled him to a life amid the wild.

"My father's quest was to retrace all the routes of the voyagers across Canada," he says. "He and my mother had five kids—I was the fourth—and he made it a point of taking one or more kids on each of his canoe trips."

For thirty years, different subsets of the family paddled down an array of secluded rivers, and for Sumner, each trip tested his mettle. Years later, he would come to appreciate these tests, believing his "suffering" played a critical role in his initiation to nature.

After enduring the canoe trips, Sumner decided to challenge himself further. At eighteen he signed up for the National Outdoor Leadership School in Lander, Wyoming, a sixty-day survival course focused on teaching people how to live off the land.

"There was a great deal of physical suffering that went along with that, too," Sumner recalls, "but I didn't mind because I was learning so much. When you go on these long canoe trips or spend that much time in the woods, you sort of get used to a certain level of suffering. And the reward is you find yourself attuned in almost a spiritual way to the beauty and diversity of landscapes. The physical hardship allows you to somehow go deeper and be more connected to the very landscape that is in part responsible for your physical suffering."

It's a statement with which Zirrer might've agreed. After all, he himself was no stranger to suffering, writing of it most pointedly in a 1959 article for the *Milwaukee Journal* nearly a decade before his death. A man in the prime of his life might've struggled to endure the blistering winter of 1958–59 in an unheated cabin, though Zirrer, seventy-two at the time, persisted nonetheless. There were hardships, of course, most notably his depletion of firewood with nearly six weeks left of winter; though thankfully, he did a better job of rationing food, even managing to share what he could with the deer mice that lived alongside him.

Despite his efforts to live as he always had, by the 1950s, even Zirrer had to admit that his once undisturbed world was now changing.

"Outside my cabin the forest looks empty and desolate," he wrote. "Before long, however, the chainsaws will be back."

His words are reminiscent of Eckelberry's during the artist's stint in the Singer Tract; in particular, their shared reference to the sound of lumbering equipment. While Eckelberry employed the sound of the "donkey engine" as a symbol of man's encroachment, Zirrer employed the sound of chainsaws to a similar end.

While Zirrer had committed himself to the wild life, in his later years, it appeared as if the wild no longer existed. Men such as he who had yearned for seclusion were finding just how difficult it had become to find any. There seemed to be no more opting out, no more life off the grid; the grid, it appeared, was now everywhere.

When I ask Sumner about the remains of Zirrer's Hayward cabin, which once resided in what is now known as the Kissick Alkaline Bog Lake State Natural Area, Sumner confirms that the foundation is still there. Or at least it was twenty years ago, the last time he himself made the trip to perform a breeding bird survey.

"The cabin itself was gone, but the foundation was very much apparent at the time. It was rectangular. There were some wooden beams on the ground where you could clearly see that there had been a structure there. They were moss covered, but it was probably ten to twelve feet wide by about . . . oh, I'd say twenty to twenty-five feet long. Whether it's still there, I don't know. Even if you were to look, I can't guarantee you'd find anything; the vegetative growth might've obscured it."

I don't need a guarantee; all I need is a clue.

Since I've already tracked down Zirrer's goshawk, I figure the least I can do is track down the place he called home; to live in his wild for a while, to stir my dying ember within.

"Maybe I'll check it out sometime," I say casually.

But there's no "maybe" about it.

PART IV

Knowing

10

Flock Together

It's much easier to prove the presence than the absence of something.
—Josh Engel, research assistant, Field Museum of Natural History, 2015

In 1999, at the conclusion of his senior year of high school, seventeen-year-old amateur birder Josh Engel of Evanston, Illinois, loaded up his parents' minivan and began a cross-country road trip in search of birds. Three equally enthusiastic birding friends accompanied him, and together, the young men traveled south, making stops in Texas and Arizona before veering west to California.

"I look back on it now and I can't believe my parents let me do it," Josh marvels during a recent phone interview. "I mean, we were just kids sleeping on picnic tables and eating cold cans of soup. But I'm still friends with a lot of the people I met on those trips," he adds. "Many are still working with birds."

Including Josh.

Today he serves as a research assistant at Chicago's Field Museum, though his travels often take him well beyond the museum's wall. A recent research project on the effects of climate change on the Albertine Rift led him from the Congo to Uganda and Rwanda, among other African nations. More recently he's joined a project in the Amazon basin, one he hopes will help him and his team better understand the genetic variation among the region's species.

The work's important, Josh explains, because the more we know about species' genetic biodiversity, the more we know about biodiversity on the whole.

"Some people think it doesn't matter which forests we protect, just that we're protecting as much as we can," Josh says. "Which, of course, is what we'd like to do. But now we know that some areas have a lot of birds that are really genetically distinct, so we can use our findings to help inform conservation groups on how best to use their resources."

For half an hour or so, Josh breaks down the scientific implications of his research (and there are indeed many of them), though throughout our conversation, I keep coming back to the image of a seventeen-year-old Josh sleeping on picnic tables and eating cold cans of soup. For me, it's proof of his passion, one realized at an early age and continuing on to this day.

After prodding, Josh regales me with some of the more memorable moments from his road trip.

Such as driving the dark highways on the Fourth of July, watching wide-eyed as one small town after another lit up the landscape with fireworks.

And the equally wondrous scene that occurred just days later: how he and his friends were asleep on their picnic tables in a Texas state park only to be woken by an armadillo rummaging directly beneath them.

Though the road trip was punctuated with various highlights, the young men's most notable sighting came in the form of an endangered Golden-cheeked Warbler.

"We woke one morning and there it was," Josh says, "a beautiful male coming to drink by a pool of water on the side of the trail. I remember seeing it and thinking, *This is fun. It's not a bad way to live your life.*"

And for the most part, it's the way he continues to live it.

Five months after our phone conversation, I make my own road trip to visit Josh at the Field Museum. He's agreed to take me behind the scenes and introduce me to a few extinct birds, the Ivory-billed Woodpecker among them.

Though my wife and young children have little interest in spending spring break amid mothballed specimen drawers, we eventually reach a compromise. In exchange for a hotel with a pool within walking distance of Navy Pier, I'll get to spend some quality time with a dead woodpecker.

And so, the morning following our swim and a ride on the Ferris wheel, we begin our walk to the Field Museum. It's hardly within walking distance, though this doesn't prevent my wife and I from taking turns pushing the stroller for a few miles along Lakefront Trail.

It's a decision we soon regret ("Why didn't we take a taxi?" my wife wonders aloud), and once my "It'll build character" line begins to wear thin, I fear a mutiny is upon me.

But in the moments prior to familial meltdown, I at last glimpse the distant columns of the Field Museum.

"Museum ho!" I call, but no one is in a laughing mood.

At least not until we're greeted by a colony of gulls, their webbed feet pitter-pattering across the paved trail as Henry welcomes them with open arms, an action the gulls smartly perceive as a threat.

"Don't chase 'em," I chide as the gulls take refuge in the water. "How would you like it if we chased you into the lake?"

Laughing, Henry assures me he'd like it a lot.

Eventually—after my son endures a fifteen-minute lecture on conservation, biodiversity, and why we don't chase anything ("Not even your sister!") into Lake Michigan—we at last arrive at the Shedd Aquarium, where I bid farewell to my already-irritable family and take refuge in the nearby Field Museum.

As I turn, Henry—who has apparently forgiven me my lecture— asks, "Are you gonna see your birdie today, Dad?"

He's been asking me this for months, the "birdie" in question being the Ivory-billed Woodpecker.

Only this time my answer is different.

"Yeah," I say, the reality setting in, "this time I actually am."

Of course, seeing an Ivory-bill specimen is hardly the same as seeing the "real thing." Though in fact the specimen *is* a real thing, or *was* a real thing, or at least is undoubtedly the closest I'll ever come to knowing the "real thing" in real life. I figured I'd already had my "closest" encounter after examining Eckelberry's sketches of that alleged last bird, though now, thanks to Josh, I'm tiptoeing a bit closer still.

Upon entering the museum, my eyes widen as I peer out at the marbled interior of Stanley Field Hall. Just ahead of me is Sue—the world's most complete T. rex fossil—and beyond her, a pair of totem poles reaching toward the vaulted ceiling.

Though the museum has just opened, the hall is already overflowing with patrons: mothers and fathers plotting their routes by way of museum maps, while hoards of schoolchildren gather round the dino. The enthusiastic rush of voices echoes throughout the cavernous hall, serving as a time machine of sorts as I remember my own past visits.

Like the time my three-year-old brother got lost in the pyramids of ancient Egypt.

And the time my parents pulled me away from the taxidermied man-eating Tsavo lions.

The museum holds so many memories for me, though I know the one that will last the longest has yet to even be made.

Dressed in jeans and a gray t-shirt, thirty-three-year-old Josh Engel meets me alongside Sue's torso.

"Hey there," I say, introducing myself. "Thank you so much. This is pretty incredible for me."

Maybe it's the dinosaur, or the mummies, or the anticipation for what's to come, but whatever the reason, Josh barely squeezes a word in before I begin prattling on about how I'm quite certain Josh has the best job in the world.

"I mean, you get to see this stuff every day," I babble. "The dinosaurs and the birds and the . . ."

The scruffy-bearded young research assistant smiles as I trail off, agreeing it's a pretty good gig.

"But there are entire days when I'm in the office," he reminds me, "entire days without actually seeing Sue or knowing the public's here.

Which is why," he continues, peering back at the crowd as we wait for the elevator, "it's nice to spend a bit of time in the hall."

But as the elevator doors open, that time comes to an end, and I watch giddily as Josh takes me where the public isn't—to the "staff-only" third floor.

A moment later the doors reopen to reveal a narrow hallway, complete with exposed pipes overhead and animal photos and relief maps framed on both sides of the walls.

He leads me past several zoology offices en route to the Rosenthal Library, where we make a brief stop to examine a rare, original copy of Audubon's double elephant folio of *Birds of America* encased behind glass.

"This is a particularly special copy," Josh explains as we peer down at the page dedicated to the Pomarine Jaeger. "Toward the end of the run, Audubon painted a few extra plates, but only three copies of the book with the extra plates exist. And this is one of them. I heard he added the plates because he was trying to paint every bird in North America," Josh continues, "and as he was going, people kept describing more and more birds. So he sort of had to scramble to get the rest of them done."

What a wonderful problem, I think. *Having too many birds rather than too few.*

He continues the tour, backtracking us into the hallway until we arrive at the bird collections room. In many ways, it resembles the other collections rooms I've seen—a cavernous space lined with drawers—except here at the Field Museum, there's at least one major difference: these particular drawers are locked.

Upon entering the room, the first specimen I see is hardly a specimen at all.

It's a bust of a Dodo, its head cocked curiously toward me.

"You don't have any of these guys, do you?" I joke, knowing full well that the bird's extinction predates modern preservation techniques.

"Unfortunately, no," Josh says, handing me a pair of purple gloves as we move toward the cabinets. "But I think we've got a few other specimens you might find interesting."

Stay calm, Hollars, I remind myself as we move toward the drawers, but even I know that's wishful thinking. How am I supposed to stay calm given the many months I'd dedicated to reading of these birds in books?

Though, in truth, my newfound enthusiasm is precisely why I'd planned this trip in the first place. I'd grown tired of turning pages in books and desperate for an authentic experience. Or at least as "authentic" an experience as one can have when dealing with long-dead birds.

Indeed, I will be momentarily spared from having to read more about what Leopold called "book-pigeons," but how much better are "specimen-drawer-pigeons" or, for my purposes, "specimen-drawer-woodpeckers"?

Admittedly, this is a less than ideal situation, but it's as ideal a situation as I can imagine under the circumstances.

At least I'm going to see them today, I remind myself. *I'm going to take a dream and turn it tangible.*

"This is sort of our show-and-tell drawer," Josh says, interrupting my thoughts and reaching for his keys. "It's what we like to show visitors."

He pulls the drawer, and the room bursts alive with color.

There is the pink of the Roseate Spoonbill, the green of the Carolina Parakeet. And nearby, an array of blue- and red-feathered birds the likes of which I've never seen. Placed belly up alongside the Carolina Parakeet is a rosy-chested male Passenger Pigeon, while in the far right corner of the drawer rests another bird—this one with an unmistakable ivory-colored bill.

"So we've got a few extinct birds in here," Josh says, pointing them out one after the other. "The Passenger Pigeon, the Carolina Parakeet, the Ivory-billed Woodpecker . . ."

There he is, I think, eyeing the bird and maintaining my composure all at once.

"So why's this the drawer you show visitors?" I ask, which seems a normal enough question, and one that buys me time to allow my heart rate to return to normal.

"We like to say the museum is a library of biodiversity," he explains. "And in the case of these birds, we're preserving remnants of biodiversity that no longer exist in the wild."

He reaches for the Ivory-bill, then the Pileated alongside it.

"For instance, if you compare these two," he begins, "you'll notice that the size is not that different. But the bill on the Ivory-bill is just gigantic, and you can see the white feathers here on the back . . ."

I nod dumbly, my once frenetic behavior having been replaced with an unexpected bashfulness. I can't explain the change except to say that I am simply humbled to be in that bird's presence, grateful to have made his acquaintance, even after his death.

And then, Josh does me one better.

"Here you go," he says, handing me the Ivory-bill.

Suddenly I am holding him, my purple gloves gripping his feathered frame with a level of care I usually reserve for my ten-month-old daughter.

"Can you . . . would you mind snapping a photo?" I ask.

Josh takes my phone and begins snapping—*click, click, click*—as I pose alongside that bird.

For better or worse, my extended photo shoot with the Ivory-bill confirms me as a fanboy of the highest order; a price I'm willing to pay. While it indeed jeopardizes my neutral reporter's tone, I imagine—given the many bird-gushing emails I'd sent him—that Josh never expected much in the way of neutrality from me anyway.

Holding that bird, I'm faced with a complicated feeling—part joy, part grief, part something bordering on the sublime. And it's my inability to give it a proper name that makes the emotion even more powerful. This is my moment of quiet reckoning, my real-life anagnorisis.

I'm in love with a bird, I realize as the camera clicks. *But I'm also mourning the bird that I love.*

And this isn't just any bird, mind you, but a bird—like so many others—with a backstory. According to the tag wrapped round his leg, this particular specimen was killed on March 13, 1883, near the Wekiva River in central Florida. His killer: a man named Charles B. Cory.

Cory, I would later learn, was a rarity in his own right. The independently wealthy nineteenth-century man traveled the world in search of birds, though by 1893 had become so proficient at acquiring them that his home could no longer hold all nineteen thousand. He donated his collection to the Field Museum—including the Ivory-bill now in my hands—and in return, was given the lifetime appointment of curator of ornithology.

I know you now, I think, staring down at the feathered mass in my hands. *Or at least some part of you.*

Eventually, I'm persuaded to return that bird to the drawer without the coaxing of security guards, and as a reward for my good behavior, Josh introduces me to a few additional birds we're not likely to see again: a pair of Labrador Ducks and, sharing their cabinet, a Great Auk.

"Look at the size of this thing," I whisper, examining the auk posed upright in the glass case.

"That's the North American equivalent of a penguin," Josh tells me. "It's the closest we get."

And it's the closest I'll ever get to see one.

"We've actually got some more Ivory-bills over here," Josh says, walking me to the opposite side of the room. He unlocks another drawer, this time revealing eight additional Ivory-bills laying claws-up, side by side. He places the drawer on a nearby table, and we dedicate a bit more time to marveling. The tags note that most of these specimens originated in Louisiana, though nothing specifically from the Singer Tract.

Yet a few of them came from the Wekiva River as well, which leads me to wonder: *Were these the relatives of the bird I'd just held in my hands?*

Though the birds' bills are certainly of note, I'm equally taken by the extreme size of their feet and claws. There's something prehistoric about them, which, given birds' shared genetic makeup with dinosaurs, makes sense. But it's more than genetics. These birds appear prehistoric to me because I've made them into ancient history in my head. Because, despite my contrary desires, I haven't allowed myself to authenticate the more recent sightings, and thus, rely upon Eckelberry's 1944 encounter as the last confirmed American sighting I can fully believe. Having been born forty years after that sighting, of course it seems like ancient history to me. After all, a lot can happen in forty years; I refer you to the decimation of the Passenger Pigeon.

Josh and I stare down at the birds in the drawer for a minute or so, until at last I speak.

"When you see these birds, what do you think about?"

"Well," he begins, "one thing that comes to mind is that hope springs eternal. I mean they became world news when we thought we'd rediscovered them. I think that goes to show there's always some flicker of hope in the back of our minds, just this little flicker that these extinct things aren't exactly extinct."

He pauses, his eyes staring hard into the drawer.

"I don't know if it's because we want to absolve ourselves from responsibility for our destruction or what, but there's always that flicker of hope that maybe a Passenger Pigeon will reappear, or an Ivory-bill . . ."

"Do you remember where you were," I ask, "when the rediscovery announcement was made?"

"Oh, I remember exactly where I was. I was at a meeting of the Evanston North Shore Bird Club to hear a friend of mine talk, and a guy got up at the beginning and said, 'This is going to be announced tomorrow: they think they've rediscovered the Ivory-billed Woodpecker.' It sent chills down my spine."

Though over time, those chills were replaced with disappointment.

"It wasn't until a little while later that I, along with everyone, began wondering what the real story was. Given all the effort that went into the search, it seems unlikely that the bird could've remained hidden. There's just no way they'd go unnoticed. Ivory-billed Woodpeckers were loud and big, and even if you didn't see them you'd see signs of them all over the forest because they rip the bark from the trees."

"So what do you think happened?" I ask. "Why did the search yield so little? Because there was nothing to find?"

"I don't know," Josh shrugs. "I guess that flicker of hope got the better of them."

But as Josh makes clear, for a time, hope got the better of him, too.

"It's much easier to prove the presence than the absence of something," he says as he slides the drawer back into the cabinet. "After all, it's pretty difficult to say with certainty that something doesn't exist."

And so, we don't say that. We don't even think it.

We just lock up the drawers and hope.

A few weeks after my trip to the Field Museum, I stumble upon a flyer for a dinner sponsored by the local chapter of the Sierra Club. The flyer informs me that the dinner doubles as an awards ceremony as well, and I'm hardly surprised to learn that this year's recipient is Steve Betchkal.

I arrive at First Congregational Church at a few minutes past 6:00 p.m., bounding up the stairs and patting a nametag to my chest. The room is already filled with fifty people or so, all of whom cluster in small groups between the rows of checkered–table clothed tables. As I drift toward the drinks, I overhear pieces of conversations, most of which have to do with the region's most pressing environmental concerns, from frac sand mining to proposed budget cuts to the state's DNR. But amid the pessimistic grumbles are smiles, too, the widest of which beams forth from the award recipient.

Wine in hand, I watch as Steve holds court in the center of the room, chatting with a few acquaintances. He towers over them, his lean frame bent slightly forward as his head bobs to the beat of the conversation. He's dressed in a violet-colored button-up and khakis, and for the first time since I've known him, there doesn't appear to be a pair of binoculars anywhere within arm's reach.

What if a bird suddenly flies in through the stained glass windows, I wonder. *What'll he do then?*

His wife, Julie, stands to his left, and during a break in the conversation, I draw her attention with a wave, introduce myself, thank her for allowing me to monopolize so much of her husband's time.

"Oh, I don't mind sharing him," Julie smiles.

"He's done so much for me," I admit. "He's taught me so much. About birds, sure, but about all kinds of things, really."

She nods knowingly, leading me to believe she's heard this line before.

"So how would you describe him?" I ask, our eyes fixed on the man in question.

"Gosh . . ." she says. "I really have no idea. He's almost . . . indescribable."

Steve turns, his ears ringing, no doubt.

"Hey!" he calls out, extending a hand. "Thanks for coming."

"No problem," I say. "I'm actually in the midst of plying your wife for information about you."

"He wants me to describe you," she informs him.

"You didn't just say 'sexy'?" he asks, his straight face giving way to a smile.

"So you ready for tonight?" I ask. "Feeling good?"

"Yeah, yeah," he shrugs, staring out at the people gathering. "I've gone over my presentation enough that I don't have to read it or anything."

"You'll be fine," Julie assures, wrapping her arm around his waist. "Besides, these people are your friends."

"We'll see . . ." Steve says, and right on cue, he's approached by the next wave of well-wishers.

I turn back to Julie, whose furrowed brow confirms she's still mulling over my initial question.

"You can think it over," I assure her. "No need to come up with an answer right now."

"I will," she agrees. "I definitely will."

At a few minutes before 6:30 we begin to take our seats.

Across the room I spot Dave Linderud, the third member of our Nelson Christmas Count team.

"Dave," I say, reintroducing myself. "B.J. Hollars, from the Count."

He pauses until a look of recognition crosses his face.

"B.J.!" he says. "Good thing you said something. I almost didn't recognize you."

"I almost didn't recognize you," I admit. "We clean up nice, I guess."

I take a seat across from him, say, "It's a big night for Steve."

"Sure is," Dave agrees. "He's such a talented guy. We're so lucky to have him here."

"Lucky to have you here, too," I say. "You've got your own depth of knowledge."

Dave's modesty is in line with Sumner's and Zirrer's.

"Well, I may have known things once," he agrees. "Problem is, these days I've forgotten more than I remember."

Over salad, pasta, and bread, our half of the table talks nature: from Chimney Swifts to Bald Eagles to waterways and hiking trails. It's good talk among good people, all of whom are acutely aware of our personal responsibilities in preserving the world we've got. But as we reach for the tiramisu our chatter comes to a close.

A hush falls over the crowd as Sierra Club member Jeff Henry takes to the podium, thanks us for coming, then begins introducing this year's recipient of the Earth Green Award.

He begins by running us through Steve's statistics: over ten thousand video stories produced for the local news, 144 articles for the local paper, a writer of books, a painter of paintings, and perhaps the most telling stat of all: 934 bird species identified throughout the world.

"Most bird watchers maintain one or maybe two bird lists," Henry explains. "For Steve, list making is part of his DNA."

As proof, he references Steve's book, *Make Birds Not War*, in which Steve dedicates "two pages with a partial list of lists he maintains."

The crowd chuckles at Henry's seemingly hyperbolic statement, though having seen these lists for myself, I nod knowingly.

Henry's introduction stretches on for nearly fifteen minutes, though even at that length, he only manages to scratch the surface of Steve Betchkal's many accomplishments. When at last called to the front of the room to accept his award, Steve offers the obligatory smile and handshake, then cracks a joke about "giving the camera what it wants" as he turns to face the videographer recording him off to the right.

But for Steve, the award is only half the honor, the other half coming in the form of his captive audience. Always a teacher, Steve asks for someone to dim the lights as he turns to a laptop to begin his Power-Point presentation.

Suddenly he is fully at ease, the confidence growing in his voice as he flips through the slides and begins his prepared remarks.

"Why did you select me to receive this award?" he asks the room. "Is it because we think alike? I can think of a thousand ways in which we think alike, but I can also think of a thousand ways in which we think differently."

This idea soon becomes the central theme of his presentation, one he'll elaborate on by way of both scientific and personal examples. He wants to "challenge our thinking," he explains, to help us to see the world beyond black and white.

"How many people in this room believe in diversity?" he asks.

Every hand shoots up.

"How many believe in justice?"

The hands remain.

"How many believe in the sanctity of life? That beauty is worth fighting for?"

Nobody moves a finger.

"And how many believe that professional athletes are paid way too much?"

The crowd laughs, and again, the hands don't budge.

"These are all things we agree on exactly," Steve says. "They're as simple as black and white."

Next, he moves into areas with less agreement, asking the audience who among us believes in Jesus Christ, Allah, the goddess.

After gathering the room's responses, he informs us that he himself is a believer in all of the aforementioned deities, though he does not consider himself a Christian, a Muslim, or a Wiccan.

"So you say to me, 'You're an intellectual coward. If you believe in all things, you believe in nothing.' But that is not gray thinking," he reminds us.

Steve urges us to take the broader view, the inclusive view, the one that allows for a greater diversity of opinion. This theory was spurred, Steve explains, when a longtime friend and birding buddy cut ties with him as a result of their differing political views.

"I want to spend time with people who think like me," the former friend informed him.

It had been a blow to Steve, one he'd first told me about on the day of our binoculars tour. Though when the story is retold in this context, I now have a better sense of Steve's strong convictions about freedom of expression. After all, his convictions had cost him a friend.

For the remainder of the presentation, Steve emphasizes the need for diverse opinions in a lecture that ranges from sponges, to ice cream, to the Portuguese man-of-war. Yet despite this range, it all somehow makes sense, a Rube Goldberg approach that indeed challenges my thinking.

Steve concludes by returning to the words of Nikos Kazantzakis, the Greek writer whose work had first influenced him in a high school classroom so many years before.

"Kazantzakis wrote that God is elevated or God is denigrated in every single one of our actions. And I think," he continues, letting the words sink in, "that this is an excellent illustration in how we might think about what we do, as well as what environmentalists might take to heart every day."

He clicks through the slides one after the next, eventually leading us to his final point.

"We see being as black or white, as heaven or hell. What is hell? For me, it's a world where people feel the need to carry guns to pretend to feel safe, where humans make a game of blowing one another up, where 7 percent of males believe rape is justifiable. And Heaven? That to me is a vital and viable systemic organism pulsing with oxygen and rain forests and singing birds—many, many birds. And they're for my children and your children—no matter whether they think alike or differently. For that, you see,"—he pauses for effect—"is black and white, not gray."

The room returns to full light, revealing a crowd mostly enlightened but also a bit bemused.

Admittedly, it's a lot to take in, a grand theory that transcends any singular environmental concern and, instead, asks every last one of us to reevaluate our worldviews.

"He must be in Mensa," I overhear a man whisper as he walks toward the church foyer.

I smile. Though I don't believe Steve is, in fact, a Mensa member, there's no doubt he probably could be. He's a freethinker, that's for sure, one whose values have been shaped by his many rewarding experiences among nature. I credit the birds most of all, the winged messengers who, for thirty-seven years, have contributed to Steve's "rebirth" as an environmentally conscious citizen.

As I stand to leave, Julie approaches me once more.

"Throughout his entire speech, I kept thinking about your question," she tells me. "About how I would describe him."

"Any breakthroughs?" I ask.

"No," she laughs. "I still don't know! He's creative and passionate and . . . he's just so many things."

I smile, think, *That's because he's not black or white, but gray.*

Though Steve Betchkal may indeed be hard to pin down, he's an open book compared to Francis Zirrer. Zirrer, who left so little behind, remains mostly a mystery for me. I can reread his letters and articles only so many times, and after a while they begin to lose meaning.

I begin to wonder, *How might I come to know him better?*

Thanks to a tip from Sumner Matteson, the answer is now obvious: I need to know his land.

In late March a buddy and I drive two hours north to Zirrer's former home in Hayward, hopeful to find some clue of the hermit's existence. Worst-case scenario, we figure we'll inhabit Zirrer's world for a while, poke around in the sedge and the tamarack as he had so many years before. And best case, maybe we'll find the remnants of his cabin, which, to my knowledge, hasn't been seen in twenty years.

We arrive at his now public land by midmorning, then lace up our boots, reach for our binoculars and camera, respectively, and strike off into the wild. The sun is up, and the wildlife's awake. Shortly after entering the bog we're greeted by a flyover courtesy of a pair of Trumpeter Swans, and then, for the next half an hour or so, play tag with a couple of Pine Siskins. Bald Eagles hover overhead, while down below, the sedge and the skunk cabbage cushion our every step.

We tromp the trails before ducking into the wilder regions, our eyes scanning the ground for any sign of Zirrer's cabin—a foundation, perhaps, or a few old boards. Though we cover the entire perimeter of the lake, all we're left with are a few pretty good guesses as to where the cabin might've been.

"You'd build a cabin here, right?" my friend asks, lowering his camera to examine the cleared mound just thirty or so feet from the water's edge.

"Oh yeah, totally," I say. "What hermit wouldn't?"

Though hardly hermits ourselves, for a moment, we embrace the nature that surrounds us.

How easy it would be, I think, *just to drift off the grid for a while.*

Of course, the thought hardly occurs to me before I realize how little truth it holds. Given my familial and professional responsibilities, "drifting off the grid"—even momentarily—would likely leave me with a wife no longer willing to indulge my unconventional "research" methods, not to mention several classrooms filled with students left scratching their heads.

What happened to Professor Hollars? one would ask, to which another would reply, *I heard he's some kind of hermit now . . .*

Zirrer's bog becomes our momentary playground, my friend and I regressing to the days of our youth when it was acceptable—encouraged, even—to disconnect and wander the woods for a while. But this is no woods, it's wilderness, and every step holds the potential for an unexpected adventure.

Not that we find any. Truth be told, by lunchtime our adventurous spirit will lead us only as far as the nearest pizza buffet.

But for the moment, we are wild men, hands on our hips as we peer out at the placid lake before us and the crown of pines beyond. It's not the most secluded place I've ever been (the power lines make sure of that), but it's nonetheless marked with an air of danger, reminding me that with enough bad luck and a subpar sense of direction (both of which I possess) we could, at least hypothetically, still manage to find ourselves a bit up a creek.

As we cut through the brush, I can't help but feel as if we're being watched. Not by humans, but by the many animals sitting in silent observation. As we bumble along, I try to imagine what the unseen creatures must think of us: the pair of humans decked out in outdoor gear and trying their best to blend in.

I wonder if Zirrer did it better, I think, and of course he must have. Not because he was less of a bumbler than we are (though he was), but because after dedicating so much time to a singular landscape, wouldn't the animals come to accept him as one of their own? Or almost one of their own? Or at least enough like them to share the space in relative peace?

Surely there was a reason the goshawks came back to Zirrer year after year. Surely there were sufficient nesting trees elsewhere. And while there is undoubtedly a scientific explanation for their continual return—one having to do with migratory patterns and food supplies, no doubt—the writer in me prefers to believe they returned to him out of something more closely resembling loyalty. After all, that's the reason I've come knocking on Zirrer's nonexistent front door—one last crack at getting to know he who is unknowable.

As expected, by hike's end I find no clues left behind. No cabin, no foundation, no secret stash of letters stored in a hollowed-out tree. Instead, I'm left only with a better sense of the many reasons why a man might opt out of the world.

Three hours in, I'm weary and, admittedly, a bit turned around as the wilderness begins to blur. Suddenly the sedge mat beneath my feet is indistinguishable from the sedge mat beneath my feet fifteen minutes prior. And the trees, just like the trees from before, differ only in their placement. To my untrained eye, this terrain looks the same in all directions, a "sameness" too easily mistaken for abundance, when in fact land like this has shrunken since Zirrer's time.

I eye the ground, the water, and try to make sense of Zirrer's home. But there's not much sense to be made. Zirrer, after all, might've lived anywhere in this bog, and since I don't know precisely where, he seems to haunt the whole landscape. It's almost as if he *is* the landscape, his echo heard in the flutter of wings and the groan of the trees' uppermost branches. I can't help but hear him in the slurping sound the muck makes as it crowds around my boots, can't help but see him, too, in the tremble of the leather-leaf.

"Ready to grab some grub?" my friend asks, snapping me back from my existential crisis.

"Sure," I agree, and within twenty minutes' time, I'm back to plucking pizza slices from beneath heat lamps.

I'll close with a story you've heard many times before.

Once upon a time there lived a bird and then that bird stopped living.

The question, though, is: What have we learned from the birds that have gone away?

For one, if renowned bird artist Roger Tory Peterson was correct in claiming that birds serve as our "ecological 'litmus paper,'" then perhaps we've learned that our planet is in trouble.

Which, I admit, is hardly breaking news.

Perhaps more alarming is this claim's obvious extension of logic: if, in fact, our planet is in trouble, then we, its human inhabitants, are too.

Whether we like it or not, we all flock together.

Whether we like it or not, we must.

As the most recent *State of the Birds Report* makes clear, bird populations continue to dwindle throughout the world. Which is certainly bad news for the birds, though it's equally concerning to the biodiversity of ecosystems in which they are a part. Perhaps nature's metaphorical Jenga tower won't collapse as a result of the extirpation of any single species, though the tower continues to wobble.

Another lesson from birds we've lost: a reminder that these trends can be reversed.

In the *State of the Birds Report*'s more optimistic moments, it notes that birds "aren't just warning signals; they give us hope."

And there are, indeed, reasons to be hopeful.

I refer you once more to Roger Tory Peterson, who in 1963 wrote somberly of the two rarest birds of North America—the Ivory-billed Woodpecker and the Eskimo Curlew—both of which were, in his opinion, "so close to the void of extinction that their existence has been questioned in recent years." He went on to describe other species on the brink: the thirty-nine Whooping Cranes that remained (though others put the population in the low twenties), as well as the forty or so California Condors. Though Peterson was correct in his assessment of the Ivory-bill and the Eskimo Curlew, over the next half century we would exceed his expectations on the fates of the Whooping Cranes and California Condors, both of which—though threatened—still exist in the wild today.

Peterson argued that there was much to learn from birds we've lost, particularly in the case of the Passenger Pigeon, whose story highlighted a simple truth: "many birds cannot adjust to man."

"If such species are to survive," Peterson continued, "man must adjust to them and take active, even drastic measures to protect them."

Which to our credit is exactly what we've begun to do.

In the case of the California Condor, the implementation of a robust recovery plan—including a captive-breeding program—took a species that was once extinct in the wild and transformed it to a population now four hundred strong.

Efforts to save the Whooping Crane proved equally successful. Though a mere twenty-one or so remained in 1941, thanks to an array of organizations committed to both migratory and nonmigratory populations, today their numbers rival the California Condors'.

As for the future of birds, Peterson appeared to be more of a realist than an optimist. Even in 1963 he knew some bird species were soon to be extinct, "not simply because modern man has made an ecological nuisance of himself" but also because some species had "reached a cul-de-sac, a dead end out of the main stream of life in a changing world."

He's right that we can't blame ourselves entirely. While we indeed have much bird blood on our hands (see: the Dodo, the Ivory-billed Woodpecker, the Passenger Pigeon), there are other extinct species, such as the Labrador Duck, for whom the burden falls in part on nature itself.

As noted previously, extinction is, indeed, a natural, biological process. The difference, though, is that over the past few hundred years, human impact has dramatically sped up that once-natural process.

Even if there is some subjectivity in determining what qualifies as "natural," might we all agree there is nothing natural about hunting the most abundant species of bird to extinction? And might we agree also that it is illogical to destroy an animal's sole remaining habitat in order to turn a short-term profit? When we do, the species in question is no longer experiencing natural selection, but something quite different. Natural selection refers to the process whereby traits that are advantageous eventually spread through a population because they give the individuals that possess them a competitive edge. In this new circumstance, individuals within a species (and possibly the whole species) are disadvantaged because, as one ecology-minded friend put it, "We want their habitat or they make for an excellent pie."

In short, our desires shape their futures.

What we often fail to realize, however, is how their futures shape our own.

Nights when sleep won't take, I often find myself returning to my basement bookshelf, scanning past my many dog-eared favorites—*Stray Feathers from a Bird Man's Desk*, *Our Amazing Birds*, *Birds of Village and Field*, *Birds of the World*, *Birds of America*, and yes, even *Bird Watching for Dummies*—until my hand instinctually reaches once more for Aldo Leopold's *A Sand County Almanac*. I turn to "On A Monument to the Pigeon" and reread the words I've read so many times.

"It is a century now since Darwin gave us the first glimpse of the origin of species. We know now what was unknown to all the preceding caravan of generations: that man is only a fellow voyager with other creatures in the Odyssey of evolution, and that his captaincy of the adventuring ship conveys the power, but not necessarily the right, to discard at will among the crew."

I breathe easier upon remembering that we're all aboard the same ship.

After all, I think as I slip back to bed, *we'd never dare sink ourselves, would we?*

I'm uncertain of the answer, though despite the sleepless nights this question has caused, it's a small price to pay for what the birds have given me. Not just in regard to their warning cries, but as a result of their beauty, too. Lately, I've grown accustomed to overlooking their splendor, sullying my encounters by pessimistically wondering, *When will we never see you again?*

But on these warm summer nights when the only stirring in the air belongs to birds, I remind myself to do better, to appreciate these fleeting creatures in the moments that we have them. Mostly these sightings take place just beyond my kitchen window, where I'm stationed at the sink, my attention split between the dishes and the bird songs drifting just beyond the glass. While working the sponge I'm always serenaded by one bird or another, some chirp or squawk that clues me in to its being there. But these days, it's not enough just to hear it, not enough to glimpse it or spot it or even see it for a moment in time.

Steve Betchkal's influence has rubbed off on me, and now I need to know each bird by name, need to stare out the window and say, "You, my friend, are a woodpecker."

Generally speaking, even I can ID a woodpecker, though I admit, from a distance, I still sometimes get my Hairies and Downies confused. But in truth, I'm grateful for the opportunity to confuse them, grateful to have two to confuse.

I only wish I could say the same of the Pileated and the Ivory-bill, though when it comes to that particular pair, I'm afraid my ID is always correct.

Still, as I scrub those dishes, I always keep an eye out for that carmine crest, that bill of ivory, that bird once deemed the "chief of his tribe."

And on my lips, I continue to hold my hopeful whisper: *Lord God, Lord God, please, Lord God, let it be you . . .*

SOURCES

This account was written from various sources, including firsthand accounts, scholarly research, and online and newspaper articles. What follows is a list of the sources I most heavily relied upon while crafting individual chapters. The sources are ordered approximately according to the information's placement within each chapter. If a source was employed multiple times throughout a chapter, I listed it only upon its initial use.

Prologue

Wikipedia, "Dodo"; Ehret interview; *Wikipedia,* "Augury"; Cokinos, *Hope;* "Extinction Crisis," Center for Biological Diversity; Vaughan, "Humans Creating Sixth Great Extinction"; Jones, "In U.S., Concerns About Environmental Threats Eases."

1. The Resurrection of the Lord God Bird

Catesby, *Natural History of Carolina;* Wilson, *American Ornithology;* Hoose, *Race to Save;* Cornell Lab of Ornithology, "Results"; Gotelli et al.,

"Specimen-Based Modeling"; Mendenhall, "Ivory-billed Woodpecker Is Extinct"; Thompson, *Bird Watching for Dummies*; Tanner, *Ivory-billed Woodpecker*; Bales, *Ghost Birds*; Cokinos, *Hope*; Saikku, "Home in the Big Forest"; Eckelberry, "Search for the Rare Ivorybill"; Darwin, *On the Origin of Species*; *Wikipedia*, "German Prisoners of War"; Muir, *My First Summer*.

2. The Death List

"James Newman Clark Bird Museum"; S. Betchkal interview, October 23, 2014; Clark Collection, University of Wisconsin–Eau Claire; Crowe, "Bird Man"; Leopold, *Sand County Almanac*; North American Bird Conservation Initiative, U.S. Committee, *State of the Birds*; Temple et al., *"Passenger Pigeon Symposium"*; Hitt, "13 Ways of Looking."

3. The Hermit and the Hawk

Department of Commerce, Bureau of the Census, "Fourteenth Census"; Schorger Papers, University of Wisconsin–Madison; Matteson, "Francis Zirrer," 61–73, 233–49; *Wikipedia*, "Takagari"; Gromme, "Goshawk"; Jewett, *Country of the Pointed Firs*; Zirrer, "Nature Lover's North Woods Diary"; Matteson, interview; Zirrer, "Great Horned Owl."

4. The Continuing Saga of the Resurrection of the Lord God Bird

Tower, "Thing with Feathers"; Niskanen, "Eyewitness Accounts"; Dickinson, "Best-Kept Secret"; U.S. Fish and Wildlife Service. *Once-Thought Extinct*; Cornell Lab of Ornithology, "Rediscovery of the Ivory-billed Woodpecker"; Cornell Lab of Ornithology, "Quotes from the Searchers"; Rohrbaugh, Lammertink, and Piorkowski, *Final Report*; Ribas, "Ivory-billed Woodpecker Search Ends"; Fitzpatrick et al., "Ivory-billed Woodpecker"; Sibley et al., "Comment"; Jackson, "Ivory-billed Woodpecker"; Blockstein, "Hope and the Lord God Bird"; Jackson, "Ivory-bill after a Decade"; Moser, "Last Ivory Bill"; Harwood, "You Can't Protect"; White, "Ghost Bird"; Hitt, "13 Ways of Looking"; Sibley, *Sibley's Birding Basics*.

5. The Life List

Davidson, "Ignazio Porro"; S. Betchkal interview, November 22, 2014; Emerson, "Nature"; Sander, "Fall of Sparrow"; *Wikipedia*, "Dusky Seaside Sparrow"; Thompson, *Bird Watching for Dummies*.

6. The Professor and the Pigeon

"Bert's Pigeon Search"; Temple et al., "Passenger Pigeon Symposium"; "Stanley Temple—Emeritus Faculty Profile," Department of Forest and Wildlife Ecology; Janik, *Short History of Wisconsin*; Leopold, *Sand County Almanac*; Schorger, *Passenger Pigeon*; Greenberg, *Feathered River across the Sky*; Greenberg, "Fate of the Passenger Pigeon"; Theodore Roosevelt to John Burroughs, May 23, 1907, Roosevelt Papers; *Wikipedia*, "Endling"; Eckelberry, "Search for the Rare Ivorybill"; McCabe, "A. W. Schorger"; Hickey, "In Memoriam."

7. The Stunning Conclusion of the Continuing Saga of the Resurrection of the Lord God Bird

Weinke interview; Pollack, "Don R. Eckelberry"; *Birds in the Hand*; Eckelberry Papers; Severson, "Memories."

8. The Christmas Count

"Christmas Bird Census"; National Audubon Society, "First Christmas Bird Count"; Chapman, "Christmas Bird-Census"; Chapman, "Camera in Nature Study"; National Audubon Society, "Number of Christmas Bird Count Circles"; S. Betchkal interview, January 3, 2015; Linderud interview; Lewis, "Birth of EPA"; Chapman, *Handbook of Birds*.

9. The Ghost of the Goshawk

Schorger Papers, UW-Madison; Gromme, "Goshawk"; Holahan interview; Zirrer, "Goshawk"; McCabe, "A. W. Schorger"; Matteson interview; Zirrer, "Nature Lover's North Woods Diary."

10. Flock Together

Engel interview, October 27, 2014; "Birds—History"; J. Betchkal interview; S. Betchkal interview, April 14, 2015; Linderud interview; Henry, "Steve Betchkal Introduction"; Peterson, *Birds*; North American Bird Conservation Initiative, U.S. Committee, *State of the Birds*; Butler, Harris, and Strobel, "Influence of Whooping Crane Population Dynamics"; Leopold, *Sand County Almanac*.

BIBLIOGRAPHY

Archives, Manuscript Materials, and Symposia

Clark, James Newman, Collection. 1867–1972. UHC249. Special Collections and Archives, McIntyre Library, University of Wisconsin–Eau Claire.

Eckelberry, Don R., Papers. Leigh Yawkey Woodson Art Museum, Wausau WI.

Roosevelt, Theodore, Papers. Manuscript Division, Library of Congress. Theodore Roosevelt Digital Library, Dickinson State University. http://www.theodorerooseveltcenter.org/Research/Diogital-Library /Record.aspx?libID=o199411.

Schorger, A.W. (Arlie William), Papers. 1951–71. University of Wisconsin–Madison Archives.

Temple, Stanley, et al. "Passenger Pigeon Symposium: From Billions to None." UW–Madison—Union South, Marquee Theater, Madison WI. November 1, 2014.

Interviews

Betchkal, Julie. Personal Interview. April 14, 2015.

Betchkal, Steve. Personal Interview. October 23, 2014; November 22, 2014; January 3, 2015; April 14, 2015.

Ehret, Dana. Personal Interview. October 9, 2014.

Engel, Josh. Personal Interview. October 27, 2014; March 26, 2015.

Holahan, Paula. Personal Interview. February 12, 2015.

Linderud, Dave. Personal Interview. January 3, 2015.

Matteson, Sumner. Personal Interview. March 12, 2015.

Weinke, Jane. Personal Interview. January 8, 2015.

Published Works

Allen, Arthur, and Paul Kellogg. "Recent Observations on the Ivory-billed Woodpecker." *Auk* 54 (1937): 164–84. Print.

Audubon, John James. *The Birds of America*. New York: MacMillan, 1942. Print.

Austin, Oliver Luther, and Arthur Singer. *Birds of the World: A Survey of the Twenty-Seven Orders and One Hundred and Fifty-Five Families.* New York: Golden, 1961. Print.

Aymar, Brandt, ed. *The Personality of the Bird*. New York: Crown, 1965. Print.

Bales, Stephen Lyn. "A Close Encounter with the Rarest Bird." *Smithsonian.* September 1, 2010. Web. March 1, 2015. http://www.smithsonian mag.com/science-nature/a-close-encounter-with-the-rarest -bird-54437868/?no-ist.

———. *Ghost Birds: Jim Tanner and the Quest for the Ivory-billed Woodpecker, 1935–1941.* Knoxville: University of Tennessee Press, 2010. Print.

"Bert's Pigeon Search." *Sesame Street.* PBS. October 12, 2010. Television.

Betchkal, Steve. *Make Birds Not War: Step by Step Instructions for Saving the World a Birder at a Time.* Eau Claire WI: Adarol, 2011. Print.

Beyer, Geo. G. "The Ivory-billed Woodpecker in Louisiana." *Auk* 17.2 (1900): 97–99. Print.

"Birds—History." *Field Museum.* Web. December 30, 2015. https:// www.fieldmuseum.org/science/research/area/birds/birds-history.

Birds in the Hand, Birds in the Bush. Perf. Donald R. Eckelberry. Grant Film Productions, circa 1970s. Film.

Blockstein, David. "Hope and the Lord God Bird." *Loon* 77 (2005): 106– 10. Web. September 1, 2014. http://moumn.org/loon/view_frame .php?block=106&year=2005.

Bond, Alexander, Keith Hobson, and Brian Branfireun. "Rapidly Increasing Methyl Mercury in Endangered Ivory Gull (*Pagophila eburnea*) Feathers Over a 130 Year Record." *Proceedings of the Royal Society B: Biological Sciences* 282 (2015). Web. https://www.researchgate.net/publication/273781827_Rapidly_increasing_methyl_mercury_in_endangered_ivory_gull_Pagophila_eburnea_feathers_over_a_130_year_record.

Burton, Robert. *Birdfeeder Handbook*. New York: Covent Garden Books, 2005. Print.

Butler, Matthew J., Grant Harris, and Bradley N. Strobel. "Influence of Whooping Crane Population Dynamics on Its Recovery and Management." *Biological Conservation* 162 (2013): 88–89. Print.

Catesby, Mark. *The Natural History of Carolina, Florida and the Bahama Islands*. London: Benjamin White, 1771. University of North Carolina Chapel Hill Library. Web. July 1, 2015. http://www2.lib.unc.edu/dc/catesby/.

Chapman, Frank M. "The Camera in Nature Study." *Current Literature* 31 (1901): 457–60. Web. December 15, 2015. https://books.google.com/books?id=-egAAAAYAAJ&pg=PA457&dq=frank+chapman+%22the+camera+in+nature+study%22&hl=en&sa=X&ved=0ahUKEwifvZqtztzLAhVrvYMKHUVvDVEQ6AEIJjAA#v=onepage&q=frank%20chapman%20%22the%20camera%20in%20nature%20study%22&f=false.

————. "A Christmas Bird-Census." *Bird-Lore* 2 (1900): 192. Web. May 1, 2015. http://www.audubon.org/sites/default/files/documents/original_cbc_mention_in_bird_lore_1900.pdf.

————. *The Economic Value of Birds to the State*. Albany NY: J. B. Lyon, 1903. Print.

————. *Handbook of Birds of Eastern North America*. New York: D. Appleton, 1920. Web. March 1, 2015. https://archive.org/details/handbookofbirdso00cha.

Chivian, E., and A. Bernstein, eds. *Sustaining Life: How Human Health Depends on Biodiversity*. Center for Health and the Global Environment. New York: Oxford University Press, 2008. Print.

"The Christmas Bird Census." *Bird-Lore*. 1901. Web. May 1, 2015. http://tx.audubon.org/sites/default/files/documents/first_birdlore_1901_nas.pdf.Cokinos, Christopher. *Hope Is the Thing with Feathers: A*

Personal Chronicle of Vanished Birds. New York: J. P. Tarcher/Putnam, 2000. Print.

Cornell Lab of Ornithology. "Behind the Scenes with the Search Team." *Rediscovering the Ivory-billed Woodpecker.* 2005. Web. January 24, 2015. http://www.birds.cornell.edu/ibwMedia/story7.htm.

————. "Historic Encounters." *Rediscovering the Ivory-billed Woodpecker.* 2014. Web. March 15, 2015. http://www.birds.cornell.edu/ibwMedia/story12.htm.

————. "Meet the Search Team." *Rediscovering the Ivory-billed Woodpecker.* 2005. Web. January 24, 2015. http://www.birds.cornell.edu /ibwMedia/story8.htm.

————. "Mobile Search Team Update." *Rediscovering the Ivory-billed Woodpecker.* 2014. Web. January 1, 2015. http://www.birds.cornell.edu /ivory/08_09stories/mst_March09.

————. "Quotes from the Searchers." *Rediscovering the Ivory-billed Woodpecker.* 2005. Web. January 24, 2015. http://www.birds.cornell.edu /ivory/pastsearches/2004_2005/searchteam0405/quotes.

————. "Rediscovery of the Ivory-billed Woodpecker and Its Conservation Implications: Dr. John W. Fitzpatrick." *Rediscovering the Ivory-billed Woodpecker.* 2014. Video clip.

————. "Results." *The Search for the Ivory-billed Woodpecker.* 2015. Web. November 6, 2015. http://www.birds.cornell.edu/ivory/evidence /segments/segments/resultsunderwing.

————. "The Slide toward Extinction." *Rediscovering the Ivory-billed Woodpecker.* 2014. Web. February 1, 2015. http://www.birds.cornell .edu/ibwMedia/story14.htm.

————. "Studying a Vanished Bird." *Rediscovering the Ivory-billed Woodpecker.* 2014. Web. February 1, 2015. http://www.birds.cornell.edu /ibwMedia/story13.htm.

Crowe, David. "'Bird Man' Left Legacy of Avian Lore." *Eau Claire (WI) Leader Telegram* June 3, 1976: Web.

Dalton, Rex. "Still Looking for That Woodpecker." *Nature* February 10, 2010: 11. Print.

Darwin, Charles. *On the Origin of Species.* 1859. New York: Signet Classics, 2003.

Davidson, Michael. "Ignazio Porro." *Molecular Expressions: Science, Optics and You.* October 17, 2004. Web. April 1, 2015. http://micro.magnet .fsu.edu/optics/timeline/people/porro.html.

Department of Commerce, Bureau of the Census. "Fourteenth Census of
the United States: 1920—Population." Ancestry.com Web. December
29, 2015.

Dickinson, Rachel. "The Best-Kept Secret." *Audubon Magazine* July 1,
2005. Web. April 2, 2015. http://archive.audubonmagazine.org/features
0507/rediscovery.html.

Di Silvestro, Roger. "Making Dollars and Sense in Ivory-Bill Country."
National Wildlife Federation. April 1, 2006. Web. April 15, 2015. https://
www.nwf.org/News-and-Magazines/National-Wildlife/Birds
/Archives/2006/Making-Dollars-and-Sense-in-Ivory-Bill-Country.aspx.

Eckelberry, Donald R. "Search for the Rare Ivorybill. *Discovery.* Ed. John
K. Terres. Philadelphia PA: Lippincott, 1961. 195–207. Print.

Emerson, Ralph Waldo. "Nature." In *Selections from Ralph Waldo Emerson.* Boston: Houghton Mifflin, 1957. 23–24. Print.

"Extinction Crisis." Center for Biological Diversity. Web. December 12,
2015. http://www.biologicaldiversity.org/programs/biodiversity
/elements_of_biodiversity/extinction_crisis/.

Farrar, Lara. "Without Proof, an Ivory-Billed Boom Goes Bust." *New York
Times* January 3, 2008: A14. Web.

Fenwick, George. "First Step." *Birder's World* August 1, 2005: 24–25. Print.

Fitzpatrick, J. W. et al. "Ivory-billed Woodpecker (*Campephilus principalis*)
Persists in Continental North America." *Science* 308.5727 (2005): 1460–62.
Web. May 21, 2015. https://www.sciencemag.org/content/308/5727/1460.

From Billions to None: The Extinction of the Passenger Pigeon. Dir. David
Mrazek. The Video Project, 2014. Film.

Fuller, Errol. *Extinct Birds.* New York: Facts on File, 1988. Print.

———. *Lost Animals: Extinction and the Photographic Record.* Princeton
NJ: Princeton University Press, 2013. Print.

Gallagher, Tim. *The Grail Bird: Hot on the Trail of the Ivory-billed Woodpecker.* Boston: Houghton Mifflin, 2005. Print.

———. *Imperial Dreams: Tracking the Imperial Woodpecker through the
Wild Sierra Madre.* New York: Atria, 2013. Print.

Ghost Bird. Dir. Scott Crocker. Small Change Productions, 2009. Film.

Gore, Al. *Earth in the Balance: Ecology and the Human Spirit.* New York:
Plume, 1993.

Gorman, James. "Deep in the Swamp, an 'Extinct' Woodpecker Lives."
New York Times April 29, 2005: A18. Web.

Gotelli, Nicholas J., et al. "Specimen-Based Modeling, Stopping Rules, and the Extinction of the Ivory-billed Woodpecker." *Conservation Biology* 26 (2011): 47–56. Print.

Greenberg, Joel. "Fate of the Passenger Pigeon Looms as a Somber Warning." *Yale Environment 360*. August 28, 2014. Web. December 12, 2015. http://e360.yale.edu/feature/fate_of_the_passenger_pigeon_looms_as _a_somber_warning/2797/.

————. *A Feathered River across the Sky: The Passenger Pigeon's Flight to Extinction*. New York: Bloomsbury, 2014. Print.

Gregory, William King. "Biographical Memoir of Frank Michler Chapman." *National Academy of Sciences Memoirs* 25 (1947). Web. http:// www.nasonline.org/publications/biographical-memoirs/memoir-pdfs /chapman-frank-m-1864-1945.pdf.

Gromme, O. J. "Goshawk (*Astur atricapillus atricapillus*) Nesting in Wisconsin." *Auk* 52.1 (1935): 15–20. Web. May 1, 2015. https://sora .unm.edu/sites/default/files/journals/auk/v052n01/p0015-p0020.pdf.

Hagner, Chuck. "Scientist Decries 'Faith-Based' Ornithology in Ivory-bill Search." *BirdWatching*. February 17, 2006. Web. May 2, 2015. http:// www.birdwatchingdaily.com/featured-stories/scientist-decries-faith -based-ornithology-in-ivory-bill-search/.

Hardy, John William. "A Tape Recording of a Possible Ivory-billed woodpecker Call." *American Birds* 29.3 (1975): 647–51. Print.

Harvey, Chelsea. "Scientists Say That 6,000 years Ago, Humans Dramatically Changed How Nature Works." *Washington Post* December 16, 2015. Web. December 16, 2015. https://www.washingtonpost.com /news/energy-environment/wp/2015/12/16/humans-dramatically -changed-how-nature-works-6000-years-ago/.

Harwood, Michael. "You Can't Protect What Isn't There." *Audubon* November 1, 1986: 108–23. Print.

Hasbrouck, Edwin. "The Present Status of the Ivory-billed woodpecker (*Campephilus principalis*)." *Auk* 8.2 (1891): 174–86. Print.

Henry, Jeff. "Steve Betchkal Introduction." Earth Green Award Dinner. Sierra Club. First Congregational Church, Eau Claire WI. April 14, 2015. Lecture.

Hickey, Joseph. "In Memoriam: Arlie William Schorger." *Auk* 90 (1973) : 664–71. Web. March 1, 2015. https://sora.unm.edu/sites/default/files /journals/auk/v090n03/p0664-p0671.pdf.

Hill, Geoffrey E. *Ivorybill Hunters: The Search for Proof in a Flooded Wilderness.* Oxford: Oxford University Press, 2007. Print.

Hitt, Jack. "13 Ways of Looking at an Ivory-billed woodpecker." *New York Times* May 7, 2006. Web. March 15, 2015. http://www.nytimes.com /2006/05/07/magazine/07woodpecker.html?pagewanted=all &_r=0.

Holsaert, Eunice. *Birds of the World: An Introduction to the Study of Birds.* New York: Simon and Schuster, 1957. Print.

Hoose, Phillip M. *The Race to Save the Lord God Bird.* New York: Farrar, Straus and Giroux, 2004. Print.

Jackson, Jerome A. *In Search of the Ivory-billed Woodpecker.* Washington DC: Smithsonian, 2004. Print.

———. "The Ivory-bill after a Decade: 20.3 Million Spent, Total Cost 'Unknown.'" *BirdWatching.* January 8, 2015. Web. December 26, 2015. http://www.birdwatchingdaily.com/blog/2015/01/08/the-ivory-bill -after-a-decade-20-3-million-spent-total-cost-unknown/.

———. "Ivory-billed Woodpecker (*Campephilus principalis*): Hope, and the Interferences of Science, Conservation, and Politics." *Auk* 123.1 (2006): 1–15. Print.

"The James Newman Clark Bird Museum." Facilities, Biology. University of Wisconsin–Eau Claire, 2012. Web. March 1, 2015. http://www.uwec .edu/academics/college-arts-sciences/departments-programs/biology /explore-opportunities/academic-facilities/bird-museum/.

Janik, Erika. *A Short History of Wisconsin.* Madison: Wisconsin Historical Society, 2010. Print.

Jewett, Sarah Orne. *The Country of the Pointed Firs, and Other Stories.* Selected and introduced by Mary Ellen Chase. New York: Norton, 1968. Print.

Jones, Jeffrey. "In U.S., Concerns about Environmental Threats Eases." *Gallup.* March 25, 2015. Web. December 5, 2015. http://www.gallup .com/poll/182105/concern-environmental-threats-eases.aspx.

Kemper, C. "In Memoriam." *Passenger Pigeon* 30.2 (1968): 67. Print.

Lemmon, Robert Stell. *Our Amazing Birds: The Little-known Facts about Their Private Lives.* Garden City NY: American Garden Guild and Doubleday, 1952. Print.

Leopold, Aldo. *A Sand County Almanac, and Sketches Here and There.* New York: Oxford University Press, 1987. Print.

Lewis, Jack. "The Birth of EPA." *EPA Journal* November 1985. Web. December 5, 2015. http://www.epa.gov/aboutepa/birth-epa.

Martin, John E. "Singer." *Rootsweb.* 2012. Web. 2015. http://www.roots web.ancestry.com/~lamadiso/articles/singer.htm.

Matteson, Sumner. "Francis Zirrer: Unheralded Naturalist of the North Woods." Parts 1–3. *Passenger Pigeon* 52.1 (1990): 61–73; 52.2 (1990) : 139–51; 52.3 (1990): 233–49. Web. 1 November 2014. http://digital .library.wisc.edu/1711.dl/EcoNatRes.PassPigeon.

McCabe, Robert. "A. W. Schorger: Naturalist and Writer." *Passenger Pigeon* 55.4 (1993): 299–309. Web. December 1, 2014. http://images .library.wisc.edu/EcoNatRes/EFacs/PassPigeon/ppv55no04/reference /econatres.pp55n04.rmccabe.pdf.

Meine, Curt. *Aldo Leopold: His Life and Work.* Madison: University of Wisconsin Press, 1988. Print.

———. *The Essential Aldo Leopold: Quotations and Commentaries.* Madison: University of Wisconsin Press, 2006. Print.

Mendenhall, Matt. "Ivory-billed Woodpecker Is Extinct, Say Two Teams of Researchers." *BirdWatching* February 2, 2012. Web. December 1, 2015. http://www.birdwatchingdaily.com/featured-stories/ivory -billed-woodpecker-extinct-say-two-teams-researchers/.

———. "20 Birds, 12 Hotspots, One Dream Trip." *Birder's World* December 2006: 50–57. Print.

Merriam, Florence. *Birds of Village and Field: A Bird Book for Beginners.* Boston: Houghton Mifflin, 1898. Print.

Moser, Don. "The Last Ivory Bill." *LIFE.* April 1972: 52–62. Print.

Muir, John. *My First Summer in the Sierra.* Books on Americana. New York: Dover, 2004. Print.

Murphy, Robert Cushman. "Frank Michler Chapman, 1864–1945." *Auk* 67.3 (1945): 307–15. Web. December 1, 2015. http://www.jstor.org /stable/4080919?seq=1#page_scan_tab_contents.

National Audubon Society. "The First Christmas Bird Count: December 25, 1900." 2010. Web. May 1, 2015. http://www.audubon.org/sites /default/files/documents/First_Christmas_Bird_Count_birdsplaces .pdf.

———. "Number of Christmas Bird Count Circles and Participants Over Time." 2008. Web. May 1, 2015. http://www.audubon.org/sites

/default/files/documents/Number_of_Christmas_Bird_Count
_circles_and_participants_over_time.pdf.

Nelson, E. W. "The Imperial Ivory-billed Woodpecker, *Campephilus impe-rialis* (Gould)." *Auk* 15.3 (1898): 217–23. Web. July 20, 2015. https://sora.unm.edu/node/6789.

Nijhuis, Michelle. "North American Birds." *Audubon* September 1, 2014: 25–32. Print.

Niskanen, Chris. "Eyewitness Accounts of Ivory-billed woodpecker from the Cache River, Arkansas." *BirdWatching* August 1, 2005: 20–23. Web. July 1, 2015. http://www.birdwatchingdaily.com/featured-stories/eyewitness-accounts-of-ivory-billed-woodpeckers/.

———. "Old Friend Found." *Birder's World* August 1, 2005: 20–23. Print.

North American Bird Conservation Initiative, U.S. Committee. *The State of the Birds: 2014 Report.* Washington DC: U.S. Department of Inte-rior, 2014. Web. October 10, 2014. http://www.stateofthebirds.org/.

Pasquier, Roger. *Watching Birds: An Introduction to Ornithology.* Boston: Houghton Mifflin, 1977. Print.

Peterson, Roger Tory. *The Birds.* New York: Time, 1963. Print.

———. *A Field Guide to the Birds: Giving Field Marks of All Species Found East of the Rockies.* 2nd ed. Boston: Houghton Mifflin, 2002. Print.

Peterson, Roger Tory, and Virginia Marie Peterson. *A Field Guide to the Birds: A Completely New Guide to All the Birds of Eastern and Central North America.* 5th ed. Boston: Houghton Mifflin, 2002. Print.

Pollack, Michael. "Don R. Eckelberry, Painter of Birds, Dies at 79." *New York Times* January 28, 2001. Web. June 1, 2015. http://www.nytimes.com/2001/01/28/nyregion/don-r-eckelberry-painter-of-birds-dies-at-79.html.

Rand, Austin Loomer. *Stray Feathers from a Bird Man's Desk.* Garden City NY: Doubleday, 1955. Print.

Ribas, Jorge. "Ivory-billed Woodpecker Search Ends." *Discovery News.* April 15, 2010. Web. June 1, 2015. http://news.discovery.com/animals/ivorybilled-woodpecker-search-ends.htm.

Rohrbaugh, Ron, Martjan Lammertink, and Martin Piorkowski. *Final Report: March 2009 Surveys for Ivory-billed Woodpecker and Bird Counts in the Fakahatchee Strand State Preserve, Florida.* 2009. Cornell Lab of Ornithol-ogy. *The Search for the Ivory-billed Woodpecker.* Web. May 17, 2016. http://

www.birds.cornell.edu/ivory/folder.2010-04-20.2993097079/2009%20
Fakahatchee%20Final%20Report1.pdf.

Saikku, Mikko. "'Home in the Big Forest': Decline of the Ivory-billed
Woodpecker and Its Habitat in the United States." In *Encountering the
Past in Nature: Essays in Environmental History*. Ed. Timo Myllyntaus
and Mikko Saikku. Rev. ed. Athens: Ohio University Press, 2001. 94–
125. Print.

Sander, Tom. "Fall of Sparrow Symbol of Man's Insensitivity To His
'Earthmates.'" *Palm Beach (FL) Sun Sentinel* June 26, 1987. Web. April
1, 2015. http://articles.sun-sentinel.com/1987-06-26/news/87022
40610_1_dusky-seaside-sparrow-habitat-species.

Schorger, A. W. *The Passenger Pigeon: Its Natural History and Extinction.*
Norman: University of Oklahoma Press, 1955. Print.

———. "Wildlife Restoration in Wisconsin." *Transactions of the Wisconsin Academy of Sciences, Arts and Letters* 51 (1962): 21–30. Print.

Scott, Walter Edwin, ed. *Silent Wings: A Memorial to the Passenger Pigeon.*
Milwaukee: Wisconsin Society for Ornithology, 2014. Print.

Severson, Frank J. "Memories from the Singer Tract." *Birding* March/April
2007: 42–47. Web. December 15, 2015. https://www.aba.org/birding
/v39n2p42.pdf.

Sibley, David. *Sibley's Birding Basics.* New York: Alfred A. Knopf, 2002. Print.

Sibley, David, et al. "Comment on 'Ivory-billed woodpecker (*Campephilus
principalis*) Persists in Continental North America.'" *Science* 311.5767
(2006): 1555. Web. May 1, 2015. http://www.sciencemag.org/content
/311/5767/1555.1.full?searchid=1&HITS=10&hits=10&resource
-type=HWCIT&maxtoshow=&RESULTFORMAT=&FIRSTIN
-DEX=0&fulltext=sibley.

"Stanley Temple—Emeritus Faculty Profile." Department of Forest and
Wildlife Ecology. University of Wisconsin–Madison. 2014. Web.
March 1, 2015. http://forestandwildlifeecology.wisc.edu/temple-stanley
-emeritus-faculty-profile.

Snyder, Noel F. R. *The Carolina Parakeet.* Princeton NJ: Princeton University Press, 2004. Print.

Snyder, Noel F. R., David E. Brown, and Kevin B. Clark. *The Travails of
Two Woodpeckers: Ivory Bills & Imperials.* Albuquerque: University of
New Mexico Press, 2009. Print.

Steinberg, Michael K. *Stalking the Ghost Bird: The Elusive Ivory-billed Woodpecker in Louisiana*. Baton Rouge: Louisiana State University Press, 2008. Print.

Swarthout, Elliott, and Ron Rohrbaugh. "Now What?" *Birder's World* August 1, 2005: 26–29. Print.

Talbot, Jeffrey, and Dean Miller. *Animals and Animal Symbols in World Culture*. New York: Cavendish Square, 2014. Print.

Tanner, James T. *The Ivory-billed Woodpecker*. New York: Dover, 1966. Print.

Temple, Stanley. "A Passion for a Pigeon." *Living Bird* (Cornell Lab of Ornithology) Summer 2015. 52–59. Print.

Thompson, Bill. *Bird Watching for Dummies*. Foster City CA: IDG Worldwide, 1997. Print.

Tower, Wells. "The Thing with Feathers." *Outside* March 1, 2006. Web. January 1, 2015.

U.S. Fish and Wildlife Service. *Once-Thought Extinct Ivory-billed Woodpecker Rediscovered in Arkansas*. Press Release. April 28, 2005. Web. May 1, 2015. http://www.fws.gov/news/ShowNews.cfm?ref=once-thought-extinct-ivory-billed-woodpecker-rediscovered-in-arkansas&ID=4697.

———. "Recovery Plan for the Ivory-billed Woodpecker (*Campephilus principalis*)." Atlanta GA: Fish and Wildlife Service, 2010. Web. May 1, 2015. https://www.fws.gov/ivorybill/pdf/IBWRecoveryPlan2010.pdf.

Vaughan, Adam. "Humans Creating Sixth Great Extinction of Animal Species, Say Scientists." *Guardian* June 19, 2015. Web. December 5, 2015. http://www.theguardian.com/environment/2015/jun/19/humans-creating-sixth-great-extinction-of-animal-species-say-scientists.

Weidensaul, Scott. *The Ghost with Trembling Wings: Science, Wishful Thinking, and the Search for Lost Species*. New York: North Point Press, 2002. Print.

Wetmore, Alexander. *Song and Garden Birds of North America*. Washington DC: National Geographic Society, 1964. Print.

White, Mel. "The Ghost Bird." *National Geographic* December 1, 2006. Web. March 1, 2015. http://ngm.nationalgeographic.com/2006/12/ivory-woodpecker/white-text.

Whitty, Julia. "Gone: Mass Extinction and the Hazards of Earth's Vanishing Biodiversity." *Mother Jones* May 1, 2007. Web. December 5, 2015. http://www.motherjones.com/environment/2007/05/gone.

Wilson, Alexander. *American Ornithology; or, The Natural History of the Birds of the United States: Illustrated with Plates, Engraved and Colored from Original Drawings Taken from Nature*. Philadelphia: Bradford and Inskeep, 1808. Web. January 1, 2015. https://archive.org/details/American ornitho2Wils.

Wikipedia. "Augury." November 27, 2015. Web. December 10, 2015.

———. "Dodo." April 23, 2016. Web. October 5, 2014.

———. "Dusky Seaside Sparrow." December 2015.

———. "Endling." March 23, 2015. Web. May 21, 2015.

———. "German Prisoners of War in the United States." November 20, 2015. Web. December 30, 2015.

———. "National Environmental Policy Act." December 3, 2015. Web. December 7, 2015.

———. "Takagari." November 12, 2015. Web. December 30, 2015.

Yarnold, David. "It's Time to Act." *Audubon* September 1, 2014: 20–23. Web. December 1, 2014. http://www.audubon.org/magazine/september-october-2014/its-time-act.

Yeoman, Barry. "From Billions to None." *Audubon* May 1, 2014: 28–33. Print.

Zirrer, Francis. "From a North Woods Diary; Nature Lover near Hayward, Wisconsin, Reports on Struggle of Birds and Animals to Find Winter Food, Shelter." *Milwaukee Journal* December 21, 1958. Print.

———. "The Goshawk." *Passenger Pigeon* 9.3 (1947): 79–94. Web. March 1, 2015. http://digicoll.library.wisc.edu/cgi-bin/EcoNatRes/EcoNatRes -idx?type=article&did=EcoNatRes.pp09n03.FZirrer&id =EcoNatRes.pp09n03&isize=M.

———. "The Great Horned Owl." *Passenger Pigeon* 18.3 (1946): 99–109. Web. March 1, 2015. http://digicoll.library.wisc.edu/cgi-bin/EcoNat Res/EcoNatRes-idx?type=article&did=EcoNatRes.pp18n03.F Zirrer&id=EcoNatRes.pp18n03&isize=M.

———. "The 'Great' Pileated Woodpecker." *Passenger Pigeon* 14.1 (1952): 9–15. Web. March 1, 2015. http://digicoll.library.wisc.edu/cgi-bin/Eco NatRes/EcoNatRes-idx?type=article&did=EcoNatRes.pp14n01.F Zirrer&id=EcoNatRes.pp14n01&isize=text.

———. "Nature Lover's North Woods Diary; Isolated Cabin Dweller Tells How He and His Bird, Animal Friends Survived Bitter Winter

in Forest near Hayward, Wisconsin; Spring Came Late This Year."
Milwaukee Journal April 21, 1959. Print.

———. "The Raven." *Passenger Pigeon* 7.3 (1945): 61–67. Web. March 1,
2015. http://digicoll.library.wisc.edu/cgi-bin/EcoNatRes/EcoNat
Res-idx?type=div&did=EcoNatRes.pp07n03.FZirrer&isize=text.